THE DOS AND DON'TS OF RESUME WRITING:

What is the best type of resume to write if you've only worked for one employer?

What style is right for you if you're a recent college grad? A homemaker returning to the paid work force?

Do you know the key words to use in job and skill descriptions?

Can you pick out the resume set-up that will catch a future employer's eye—and the set-up that will turn him off?

Do you know how to design a resume to cover gaps in your work record?

What are the most effective ways to write a winning cover letter?

The answers to all these vital questions can be found in this, your complete guide to successful job-hunting. RESUMES THAT WORK is a gold mine of advice, information, and inspiration, combining dozens of model resumes and cover letters with a Personal Qualifications Worksheet, and important tips on how to tailor any resume to your specific needs or special job requirements. Whether you're looking for your very first job or trying to land a better one, it's the only resume guide you'll ever need!

TOM COWAN is a professional writer with a wide range of books to his credit.

S0-BOT-913

RESUMES THAT WORK

TOM COWAN

A PLUME BOOK

NEW AMERICAN LIBRARY

NEW YORK AND SCARBOROUGH, ONTARIO

NAL BOOKS ARE AVAILABLE AT QUANTITY DISCOUNTS
WHEN USED TO PROMOTE PRODUCTS OR SERVICES. FOR
INFORMATION, PLEASE WRITE TO PREMIUM MARKETING
DIVISION, NEW AMERICAN LIBRARY,
1633 BROADWAY, NEW YORK, NEW YORK 10019.

Copyright © 1983 by Tom Cowan

All rights reserved.

Library of Congress Cataloging in Publication Data

Cowan, Thomas Dale.
    Resumes that work.

    1. Résumés (Employment)   I. Title.
HF5383.C68   1983   650.1′4   83-8332
ISBN 0-452-25455-8

PLUME TRADEMARK REG. U.S. PAT. OFF. AND FOREIGN COUNTRIES
REG. TRADEMARK—MARCA REGISTRADA
HECHO EN HARRISONBURG, VA., U.S.A.

SIGNET, SIGNET CLASSIC, MENTOR, ONYX, PLUME,
MERIDIAN and NAL BOOKS are published *in the United States* by NAL
PENGUIN INC., 1633 Broadway, New York, New York 10019, *in
Canada* by The New American Library of Canada Limited, 81 Mack
Avenue, Scarborough, Ontario M1L 1M8

First Printing, October, 1983

6 7 8 9 10 11 12 13 14

PRINTED IN THE UNITED STATES OF AMERICA

CONTENTS

RESUMES
THAT WORK

INTRODUCTION: THREE TYPES OF JOB-SEEKERS

Most people hate writing resumes. It's aggravating work, and it's worrisome, especially when you consider what hangs in the balance—a job! Whether you've worked twenty years and have written several resumes or whether you're seeking your first job, putting your qualifications down on paper—neatly, clearly, in a well organized way, and following a resume format—is always a tedious task. For everyone.

But there are three kinds of people who find this task especially difficult, and you may be one of them. Who are they?

People hunting for their first jobs: such as recent high school or college graduates, women entering the job world after a marriage and/or child rearing, ex-military personnel, people leaving religious orders.

People making their first job change: that is, workers with basically one job behind them, usually of short duration, a matter of four or five years at most, and now hunting for their second job in the same field.

Career-changers: these are people with a longer work history, ten to fifteen years or more, people in their thirties or early forties, who feel it is time to change careers or go into some related field where they can utilize the skills and experiences they have acquired in their first career, which may have consisted of several different jobs.

If you are one of these three types of job-seekers, you are in a unique situation that creates a unique—and tricky—problem in writing your resume.

As a first-job-seeker, you have little or no actual employment record to display on a resume.

So how do you fill up the page? Are you a second-job-seeker with only a few years' experience? How can you arrange that experience and word it on a resume so that it will convince a potential employer to hire you, preferably at a higher level or position than your current one? If you are a career-changer, you must carefully assess your skills, expertise, and previous accomplishments, and persuade an employer that your background, even though in a different field, is transferable and valuable to the new career.

Now if you are in one of these predicaments, you will find it even more frustrating for yet another reason. Unlike a seasoned worker who has written three or four successful resumes already, you will not have had much practice at writing resumes for your unique situation. Furthermore, you may have no model resumes to follow, and you may not know enough people (or anyone!) in your field to go to for advice.

This book is the answer to your dilemma.

HOW THIS BOOK IS ORGANIZED

In addition to addressing three particular types of job-seekers, you will find our book is organized around **major fields of work,** rather than isolated occupations arranged alphabetically. This means that you will find three, four, or more resume samples for each profession, rather than just one or two as is the case in most resume guides. For example, there are five sample resumes under "Advertising," four under "Law," and ten under "Health Care." We have found that if you read resumes written by others in your field, even if they are for different positions or levels, you will often discover ideas for your own resume: key words to use, special skills you have not previously considered, successful ways to phrase your professional experience.

For example, a secretary reading the resume of an "office manager" may discover that his or her own duties included office management responsibilities. If so, the secretary's resume might include a section entitled "Office Management Skills." We strongly encourage you, therefore, to read all the resumes in the general field for which you are writing a particular resume. You may actually discover that you are qualified to apply for a job you had never even considered!

Whichever of the three types of job-seekers you are, whatever your profession, you will find that one of the three basic resume types presented in this book will display qualifications in the best light. Some resume guides ask you to select from as many as ten different types! But why complicate matters when three basics (or a combination of them) will be perfect for your unique situation?

You will learn the basic types shortly, what distinguishes each from the others, how to design them, and—most important—how to determine which one is best for you. Deciding this is easier with our guide because with more than one resume in each field, you can see how the same experiences can be organized to fit different types of resumes. And just as we suggest you read all the sample resumes in your field, we advise that you use the handy "Cross-Reference Index" to read through all the resumes written in the style you have chosen for your own.

In addition, the "Cross-Reference Section" is also indexed according to *types of job-seekers*. So no matter whether you are seeking your first job, making your second job-change, or are a career-changer, you will be able to locate many sample resumes written for people in your special situation. Reading them will give you insights and helpful ideas for your own resume.

PART I

Getting Ready to Write Your Resume

YOUR PERSONAL QUALIFICATIONS WORK-SHEET

The first step in designing a resume is to collect your qualifications. Collect them? Yes, they've been scattered across the years of your life, and they need to be rounded up and put in one spot so you know what they are and so they are handy for you to use. In other words, your resume will consist of *data,* and the data base should be a complete inventory of everything that qualifies you for a job.

The following pages are a work-sheet on which to collect the information that will become your qualifications when placed on a resume page. Do not underestimate your experience. As you fill out the work-sheet, include all work, education, and volunteer activities that you can remember *even if they do not seem immediately related to the job you are seeking.* Later you may realize that a part-time job, or a volunteer position with a club, or a hobby you pursued ten years ago taught you skills and gave you experience that you can now display on a resume as a job qualification.

Remember that you may need to write other resumes in the future, some for different jobs than the one you are currently applying for. Keep a copy of your work-sheet and update it as you add more work and educational experiences to your life.

Many of the fill-in blanks on the work-sheet are self-explanatory, but here are some guidelines to keep you from omitting crucial information.

High School and College
When you think about the clubs and extracurricular activities you took part in, consider espe-

cially the ones that allowed you to be creative or show initiative or assume a role of leadership: for example, "chaired fund-raising committee," "dealt directly with school authorities for permissions and approval," "convinced other students to take part." Remember, you are searching your past for skills, talents, and experiences that will single you out from the crowd and make you a valuable person to hire.

College and Graduate School
If you had special experiences because of an internship or work-study program, write a brief description of them on your work-sheet. Again, look for examples of creativity, initiative, or leadership. If you are a recent college graduate, you may be able to list your internship work as a part-time job: for example, "journalism internship: wrote and edited copy for evening news program with local TV show," "nursing internship: assistant floor nurse, 50 hours of operating-room experience."

Early Part-time and Volunteer Jobs
This section is primarily for jobs you held during high school and college. However, if you have never worked full-time, such as a housewife or ex-military person, you may use this section for your part-time jobs. There is a later section in the work-sheet for your community and volunteer work.

In general, early part-time and volunteer work experiences can cover a wide range of activities: summer jobs, such as camp counselor or pool lifeguard; part-time grocery clerk while in high school; weekend jobs at local movie theaters or retail selling at a department store. Include all volunteer work for organizations and clubs: e.g., candy-stripers, political canvassing, organizing meetings or socials, typing up notices, telephoning members, leading discussions. Describe each of these jobs in enough detail that you recognize your achievements and accomplishments and can list the skills and knowledge you learned in them: for example, ''personal relations,'' ''public speaking,'' ''typing and ditto machine,'' ''organize and supervise ten people,'' ''deal with customers,'' ''entertain children.'' Don't overlook anything. Use extra paper if you need to. The points you list here may be the qualifications that land you some future job.

Full-time Employment
As with early part-time and volunteer jobs, you will want to list every accomplishment, skill, and area of expertise. In this section, however, be *even more precise in describing the duties and responsibilities* you assumed in each job. Eventually some or all of these points will be reworded and included on your resume.

Professional Memberships
This section is for people who belong to professional associations and organizations, such as American Teachers Association, American Bar Association, Organization of Psychiatric Nurses, American Writers Guild, etc. Don't overlook clubs and organizations you belong to that are not related to your current profession. For instance, you might be a grade-school teacher who belongs to the American Camping Association because you work at summer camps. Also include national honor societies, such as Phi Beta Kappa.

Community Service/Volunteer Activities
Include here all the local clubs, such as neighborhood groups, PTA, Junior League, any social service organization. Then list national organizations, such as YMCA, Scouts, Sierra Club. Remember, in cases such as the Sierra Club, you may belong to a national organization by virtue of subscribing to its magazine.

Be sure to make connections between ''activities'' and ''skills'': for example, if you ''chaired a committee,'' you probably learned such skills as ''supervision,'' ''public speaking,'' ''discussion leading'' as well as interpersonal skills like ''getting along with people,'' ''seeing others' points of view,'' ''gaining others' confidence.''

Military Service
If you were in the military, list skills you learned, such as surveying, cooking, running a commissary, construction work, radio operating.

Hobbies/Interests
Some of these may be listed under community service and volunteer activities, such as camping, playing with local symphony orchestra, belonging to little theater group. But this section should also include all your private or nonsocial interests, such as sewing, cooking, reading, movies, jogging. Many skills related to hobbies are physical: stamina, strength, agility, dexterity, sense of balance. Some are aesthetic: design, color, arrangement, structure. Some are intellectual: understanding, insight, knowledge. Don't underestimate your talents!

YOUR QUALIFICATIONS WORK-SHEET

EDUCATION
High School (name, city, state):_____

    Graduation Date:_____

    Major Studies:_____

    Honors/Awards/Class Standing:_____

    _____

    Clubs and Extracurricular Activities:_____

    _____

Offices Held:_____

Special Accomplishments:_____

_____

College (name, city, state):_____

   Graduation Date:_____

   Degree and Major Field of Study:_____

   Internships/Fieldwork Related to Degree:_____

   _____

   _____

   Honors/Awards/Class Standing:_____

   _____

   Clubs/Extracurricular Activities:_____

   _____

   _____

     Offices Held:_____

   _____

   Special Accomplishments:_____

   _____

Postgraduate/Professional Education (name, city, state):_____

_____

   Graduation Date or Dates Attended:_____

   Degree/Certification/License:_____

   Major Field of Study:_____

   Internships/Fieldwork Related to Profession:_____

   _____

   Honors/Awards/Class Standing:_____

   _____

   Clubs/Extracurricular Activities:_____

   _____

     Offices Held:_____

   _____

   Special Accomplishments:_____

   _____

WORK EXPERIENCE

Early/Part-time/Volunteer Jobs:

   Employer (name, city, state):_____

     Dates of Employment:_____

     Position or Job Title:_____

     Duties/Responsibilities:_____

     _____

     _____

Accomplishments/Achievements:_____
_____
_____

Skills Learned:_____
_____
_____

Supervisor:_____

Employer (name, city, state):_____
    Dates of Employment:_____
    Position or Job Title:_____
    Duties/Responsibilities:_____
_____

Accomplishments/Achievements:_____
_____
_____

Skills Learned:_____
_____
_____

Supervisor:_____

Employer (name, city, state):_____
    Dates of Employment:_____
    Position or Job Title:_____
    Duties/Responsibilities:_____
_____

Accomplishments/Achievements:_____
_____
_____

Skills Learned:_____
_____
_____

Supervisor:_____

Employer (name, city, state):_____
    Dates of Employment:_____
    Position or Job Title:_____
    Duties/Responsibilities:_____
_____
_____

Accomplishments/Achievements:_____

_____

_____

Skills Learned:_____

_____

_____

Supervisor:_____

Full-time Employment:

    Employer (name, city, state):_____

        Dates of Employment:_____

        Position or Job Title:_____

           Promotions:_____

        On-Job Training:_____

           Skills Learned:_____

_____

        Duties/Responsibilities:_____

_____

_____

        Skills/Areas of Knowledge/Expertise Acquired:_____

_____

_____

_____

        Accomplishments/Achievements:_____

_____

_____

        Supervisor:_____

    Employer (name, city, state):_____

        Dates of Employment:_____

        Position or Job Title:_____

           Promotions:_____

        On-Job Training:_____

           Skills Learned:_____

_____

        Duties/Responsibilities:_____

_____

_____

        Skills/Areas of Knowledge/Expertise Acquired:_____

_____

_____

_____

Accomplishments/Achievements:_____

_____

_____

Supervisor:_____

Employer (name, city, state):_____
    Dates of Employment:_____
    Position or Job Title:_____
        Promotions:_____
    On-Job Training:_____
        Skills Learned:_____

Duties/Responsibilities:_____

_____

_____

Skills/Areas of Knowledge/Expertise Acquired:_____

_____

_____

_____

Accomplishments/Achievements:_____

_____

_____

Supervisor:_____

Employer (name, city, state):_____
    Dates of Employment:_____
    Position or Job Title:_____
        Promotions:_____
    On-Job Training:_____
        Skills Learned:_____

Duties/Responsibilities:_____

_____

_____

Skills/Areas of Knowledge/Expertise Acquired:_____

_____

_____

_____

Accomplishments/Achievements:_____

_____

_____

Supervisor:_____

Professional Memberships:

Organization:_____

    Dates:_____

    Offices Held:_____

    Duties/Responsibilities:_____

    _____

    Skills Acquired:_____

    _____

Organization:_____

    Dates:_____

    Offices Held:_____

    Duties/Responsibilities:_____

    _____

    Skills Acquired:_____

    _____

Organization:_____

    Dates:_____

    Offices Held:_____

    Duties/Responsibilities:_____

    _____

    Skills Acquired:_____

    _____

Organization:_____

    Dates:_____

    Offices Held:_____

    Duties/Responsibilities:_____

    _____

    Skills Acquired:_____

    _____

Certification:

    License_____ Date Awarded:_____

    License_____ Date Awarded:_____

    Certification_____ Date Awarded:_____

References:

    Name:_____

    Professional Relationship to You:_____

Title at Company/School:_____

Address/Phone Number:_____

Name:_____

Professional Relationship to You:_____

Title at Company/School:_____

Address/Phone Number:_____

Name:_____

Professional Relationship to You:_____

Title at Company/School:_____

Address/Phone Number:_____

Name:_____

Professional Relationship to You:_____

Title at Company/School:_____

Address/Phone Number:_____

Name:_____

Professional Relationship to You:_____

Title at Company/School:_____

Address/Phone Number:_____

Name:_____

Professional Relationship to You:_____

Title at Company/School:_____

Address/Phone Number:_____

COMMUNITY SERVICE/VOLUNTEER ACTIVITIES

Name of Organization:_____

City/State:_____

Dates:_____

Activities You Engaged In:_____

_____

_____

Offices Held:_____

_____

Skills/Knowledge Acquired:_____

_____

_____

Name of Organization:_____

    City/State:_____

    Dates:_____

    Activities You Engaged In:_____

    _____

    _____

    Offices Held:_____

    _____

    Skills/Knowledge Acquired:_____

    _____

    _____

Name of Organization:_____

    City/State:_____

    Dates:_____

    Activities You Engaged In:_____

    _____

    _____

    Offices Held:_____

    _____

    Skills/Knowledge Acquired:_____

    _____

    _____

Name of Organization:_____

    City/State:_____

    Dates:_____

    Activities You Engaged In:_____

    _____

    Offices Held:_____

    _____

    Skills/Knowledge Acquired:_____

    _____

    _____

Name of Organization:_____

    City/State:_____

    Dates:_____

    Activities You Engaged In:_____

    _____

    _____

Offices Held:_____

_____

Skills/Knowledge Acquired:_____

_____

_____

MILITARY SERVICE
Branch of Military:_____

Dates:_____

Stationed:_____

Rank:_____

Special Training/Experience:_____

_____

_____

Skills/Knowledge Acquired:_____

_____

_____

HOBBIES/INTERESTS
Hobby/Interest:_____

Skills Needed/Learned:_____

_____

Hobby/Interest:_____

Skills Needed/Learned:_____

_____

Hobby/Interest:_____

Skills Needed/Learned:_____

_____

Hobby/Interest:_____

Skills Needed/Learned:_____

_____

Hobby/Interest:_____

Skills Needed/Learned:_____

_____

Hobby/Interest:_____

Skills Needed/Learned:_____

_____

RESUMES: TYPES, FORMATS, AND STYLES

THE THREE BASIC TYPES OF RESUMES

Many people with a long work history could write three resumes right now—one in each of the three basic types. It is all a matter of emphasis and arrangement. But you who have very little experience or who are changing careers need to select the type that best displays what you can bring to a new job. Here are the three basic types and what each has to offer you.

The Skill-based Resume

A skill-based resume is organized around the *skills, areas of knowledge,* and *know-how* you have acquired in your present job or over several years in different positions, or even from volunteer work, education courses, and early part-time jobs. A skill-based resume is excellent for those who possess an impressive number of skills after only a few years of work or a series of part-time jobs. Career-changers should use this type of resume to demonstrate that they have skills that can be transferred to other areas.

A skill-based resume also lends itself to a format (layout) that can cover up a spotty work record or a history of frequent job change that might suggest instability.

General characteristics of a skill-based resume:

1. Skills should be listed or categorized to clearly display your qualifications for the job position you are seeking.
2. Skills should be briefly analyzed or described. For example, "supervision" should indicate how many people you supervised and what functions they performed; "interviewing" should state whom you interviewed and for what purpose; "writing and research" should state the kinds of information researched, the sources used, what format the written material took, and so forth.
3. Employers and dates of employment should appear after the section cataloging your skills. It is not necessary to relate particular skills to particular employers.
4. Dates can sometimes be omitted. Even earlier jobs can be left off if they have not contributed to the cluster of skills you are emphasizing.

A sample of a skill-based resume appears on page 16.

JACK EDWARDS   381 Pacific Avenue   New York, NY 10017   (212) 949-2237

Job Objective: Video Producer

Video Production

—Proposed courses aimed at business, government, professional, and consumer markets
—Interviewed, hired, and supervised consultants, writers, directors, and crew
—Developed production budgets, formats, and schedules
—Monitored production and editing of videotape masters
—Projects include: Communication Skills, Time Management, Strategic Selling, Executive Development

Writing and Research

—Researched and wrote leaders' manuals and participants' manuals for use with instructional video courses
—Researched and developed subject matter content for video productions
—Wrote and edited scripts for video productions
—Composed workbooks, discussion guides and essays for adult education classes
—Wrote and edited nonfiction manuscripts for publishers
—Researched and reported on antique collections and collectors for an encyclopedia
—Generated advertising copy and promotional materials
—Projects include: The Art of the Plate, A Guide to Premarital Counseling, The Encyclopedia of Collectibles, Time Management, Performance Appraisal for Managers, Active Listening, Strategic Selling

Teaching

—Edited and evaluated others' research and writing
—Designed and taught composition, literature, creative writing, grammar, journalism, and film courses
—Sponsored and edited campus newspapers and magazines
—Evaluated and determined book selection

Library Science

—Researched and reported on topics submitted by staff and patrons
—Administered reserve and reference system among main library and 21 branches
—Evaluated collection and aided in determining book acquisitions

Work Experience

4/80 to present	Time Video Associates (NYC)	Associate Producer
8/79 to 4/80	River Communications (NYC)	Free-lance Writer
	Dalton Press (NYC)	
3/78 to 8/79	Philadelphia Public Library (PA)	Librarian
1/77 to 1/78	Liberty State Community College (PA)	Instructor
8/71 to 9/76	Keystone State University (PA)	Instructor

Education

A.B., English and History, Columbia College, NYC, 1967
M.A., English, Boston University, Boston, MA, 1971

The skill-based resume can be used to great advantage by recent college graduates, former wives or mothers, ex-military personnel—anyone who may have picked up skills in college courses, part-time work, summer jobs, volunteer organizations, etc. This type of resume is also beneficial for career-changers who must convince employers that they have the skills required for a field in which they have not previously worked.

The Functional Resume

On a functional resume the emphasis is on the *positions* you have held and the *titles* of your jobs so that the reader immediately sees what you have *done*.

There are several advantages to this type of resume. First, it can indicate that, although you may have worked for only one employer, you have actually performed a variety of duties and tasks. It can also show quite clearly that you have advanced from lower positions to higher ones, that you have a consistent record of promotion. This type of resume can also be used by a person whose official title or position involved duties not normally associated with it. In other words, if your official title is ''secretary'' but you actually *functioned* as a bookkeeper, receptionist, and assistant office manager, a functional resume will let you list all of these and highlight them to give a potential employer a more accurate picture of your work history. Lastly, the functional resume is perfect for people who have held a variety of part-time or volunteer jobs or worked at agencies or businesses which in themselves are not very impressive. If *what you did* is more impressive than where you worked, use the functional resume. For example, ''restaurant manager'' or ''chief cashier'' may be more important to emphasize than ''The Hungry Ox,'' a restaurant that may have no reference to a potential employer in another city. It also clearly states that you were not a waiter or a busser, and (if need be) can conceal the fact that you were only a *part-time* restaurant manager or cashier.

General characteristics of a functional resume:

1. Use occupational *nouns* that describe you or your position, such as, ''typesetter,'' ''layout artist,'' ''teacher,'' ''assistant branch manager,'' ''department head.''
2. Although it is traditional that you begin with your most recent position and work backward, this is not a hard and fast rule for the functional resume. You should begin with the positions most directly related to your job objectives even though they are not the most recent.
3. Each position should be explained in detail, highlighting duties, responsibilities, skills, and unique accomplishments.
4. Positions that are not directly related to the job objective or that have contributed very little to your present position can be omitted or listed with less detail.
5. Employers and dates are included but in less conspicuous places, usually after the position or title, or at the end of each job description.

A sample of a functional resume appears on page 18.

Brandy Castleman
4503 Palomina Grove
Los Angeles, CA 90023
(213)454-1132

Job Objective: Television producer

Experience:

PRODUCTION COORDINATOR
"The Days of Yesteryear,"
NBC-TV, Dorothy Franklin,
Producer

script-outline continuity, editing, story-line input, technical research, monthly story synopses, 1980 Daytime Emmy Awards Coordinator, montage editing for promotional interviews, casting, in-studio photo session supervisor, press party organizer

(Mar. '80-Present)

CASTING ASSISTANT
"The Days of Yesteryear,"
NBC-TV, Sarah Taub, Casting Director

daily cast calls, extra casting, fan mail, payroll, cast call sheets, AFTRA records

(July '79-Mar. '80)

ADMINISTRATIVE ASSISTANT
NBC Daytime and Children's
Programs, Cynthia Marlboro,
Director

on-air coordinator: "The Days of Yesteryear" and "The World of Science," literary sub-missions, heavy contact with producers and packagers, correspondence

(Sept. '78-June '79)

PAGE
NBC Guest Relations
Sidney Bettleman, Director

special assignments throughout the network: photo, programming, press relations

(Nov. '77-Sept. '78)

ASSISTANT PRESS AGENT
Packaging Enterprises, Inc.
Thomas Daly, President

promotional accounts, special promotions, press conference/opening night coordinator, television/print interview scheduling and supervision

(Aug. '75-Nov. '77)

ASSISTANT PRODUCTION MANAGER
Cinema Associates, Inc.,
Melissa Cartwell, Production Manager

on-location schedule planning and follow-up

(June '75-Aug. '75)

Education:
Loyola University, Chicago, IL

B.A. in Speech Communications
Cum laude
Phi Beta Kappa

The functional resume is recommended for all three types of job-hunters because it lets you emphasize the duties and responsibilities you have performed even though they were part-time or volunteer, and it can clearly show that you are prepared for the job you now seek even if that job is at a higher level than your current one or in a completely different field.

The Chronological Resume

In a chronological resume the emphasis is on *employers* and *dates of employment*. What first strikes the reader's eye is the companies you have worked for and the years you worked there.

Obviously this type of resume may not be very helpful for you if you are a first- or second-job-seeker who has not worked for many companies. But we include it for several reasons. First, it is the most basic and most traditional form of resume. Second, it is suitable for first- and second-job-seekers if you *have held a number of part-time or volunteer jobs* you wish to emphasize on your resume. Third, if you are a career-changer, it lets you call attention to prestigious or well-respected companies or organizations for whom you may have worked in the past.

For example, a wife or mother who has done volunteer work for the Junior League of her city or a well-known hospital or school may want to emphasize that fact by means of a chronological resume.

General characteristics of the chronological resume:

1. List the most recent job first and work backward to your first job.

2. Write brief descriptions or explanations of these jobs, but only detail the last two or three jobs, those covering the last ten or twelve years of your working life.

3. Pare down descriptions of very early jobs or ones that were not directly preparatory for the job you are seeking.

4. Do not repeat a job description for an earlier job if you have already explained it for a more recent one.

5. If your profession is one that is self-explanatory (i.e., one that does not allow a lot of room for variety or innovative duties; the kind that when you tell someone what you *are,* they usually don't ask what it is you *do),* do not detail minor or routine duties. Rather emphasize major responsibilities and unusual accomplishments.

6. Dates of employment do not need to include the month and day. Years are sufficient.

A sample of a chronological resume appears on page 20.

In summary, you might think of the three types of resumes in this way: a chronological resume highlights *where you have worked and when,* a functional resume focuses on *what you have done in those jobs,* and the skill-based resume indicates *what you have learned and what abilities you can bring to a new job.*

It is conceivable that your personal work record could be organized along any or all of the three basic types. What you must decide is which type will present your background and capabilities in the best light for the job you are seeking. Much of your decision depends on which type of job-seeker you are: a first-job-seeker, a second-job-seeker, or a career-changer.

Michael Dunning
6593 Oakland Avenue
San Francisco, CA 94122
(415) 676-1149

Job Objective: Public Relations Adviser

Employment

1977-Present

LITHO GRAPHICS AND DESIGN, SAN FRANCISCO
Client representative for major accounts of a printing
concern. Made presentations of company portfolio and
client projects. Consulted clients on technical problems.
Wrote effective sales promotion letters. Researched
and arranged meetings with new clients. Increased
sales volume 50 per cent.

1975-1977

CESAR'S PALACE INC., LAS VEGAS, NV
Producer and broadcast copy chief. Produced 40 TV commercials
and over 100 radio spots. Active in all phases of
broadcast production: management, shooting, recording,
editing. Created award-winning sales promotion campaigns.
Wrote jingles, scripts, lyrics, and advertising proposals.
Supervised writers, artists, and production staff

1974-1975

CARRINGTON FAMILY AND ASSOCIATES, SAN FRANCISCO
Special project director for Nicholas Carrington, responsible
for the thousands of professional and personal communications
initiated by Mr. Carrington's gubernatorial nomination.
Supervised writers and researchers. Established and
maintained information retrieval systems.

1973-1974

SAN FRANCISCO CITY BOARD OF PLANNERS
Assistant to the executive director. Organized executive
director's projects. Extensive written and oral communication
with public.

1972-1973

CALIFORNIA STUDY COMMISSION FOR SAN FRANCISCO
Editor and project coordinator. Edited commission reports.
Coordinated publication of reports.

Education

M.A. in Public Relations and Political Science   1972
    University of California at Los Angeles

B.A. in Journalism   1969
    Santa Rosa College, Santa Rosa, CA

For first-job-seekers we recommend the skill-based resume because it calls least attention to the fact that you have not previously been employed and puts the focus on what you *can* do for an employer.

Second-job-seekers can benefit either from the functional resume or the skill-based resume. You might also use the chronological resume if, in fact, you have held earlier part-time jobs that you want to call attention to or your current position is with a prestigious company.

For career-changers the most obvious type is the skill-based resume, since your success at changing careers depends on having the skills to transfer to a new field. However, if in your present career you have held various jobs that would impress a potential employer, perhaps the functional or even chronological type of resume should be your choice.

Sound confusing? It really isn't.

The important point to remember is this: *there are no unbreakable rules about the type of resume you should write.* Indeed, many of the most effective resumes are a combination of the three basics. For example, you may want to begin your resume with emphasis on skills but also point out the positions or titles you have held. On every resume there are several sections or blocks of information, and as you read the samples in this book you will notice that sometimes a ''functional'' resume has a strong ''skills'' emphasis to it, or that a ''chronological'' resume includes a listing of functions (job titles, positions).

A resume is a very personal document and you should feel free to play around with the various types in order to design the best resume for your purpose.

Two Important Resume Features

No matter which type of resume or combination you choose, there are two features that employers look for: *job descriptions* and *particular accomplishments*. Each of these—or both—can be worked into any type of resume.

A job description briefly lists the major duties and responsibilities that you were assigned in a specific job. You will see that very seldom do any of the sample resumes merely state the position without some explanation of what it entailed. In fact, it is to your advantage to describe your jobs to let the reader know the major tasks you performed.

Particular accomplishments are the exceptionally noteworthy achievements for which you were responsible. If you tripled sales for your company in six months, you should say so. If under your supervision, personnel turnover decreased by 25 percent, be proud of it and put it on your resume. You need not, however, include every accomplishment, only the more significant ones and those that relate directly to the job you are applying for. Don't list too many. You don't want the reader to suspect that in reality they were not all that exceptional and you are trying to make up for quality with quantity. If indeed you have many achievements to your credit, you can discuss the others in the interview.

Remember that some jobs by their very nature do not allow enough personal initiative to produce outstanding accomplishments. If yours is this type, your accomplishment then is a steady, loyal, successful completion of your duties. This in itself is something to be proud of and can be indicated on the resume by using key words, such as ''consistently,'' ''regularly,'' and ''successfully'' in your job descriptions.

Keep in mind that job descriptions and accomplishments should be brief and to the point. Some people's job situations are more self-explanatory than others. For example, a person who has been a bookkeeper for ten years does not have to go into as much detail about duties as a person who has worked as a bookkeeper for only two years and is now seeking his or her second job. An employer will assume that in ten years the older bookkeeper has acquired the skills and has performed the major activities of general bookkeeping. On the other hand, the second-job-seeker will want to show clearly that even after only one job of short duration, his or her bookkeeping skills qualify for the new job under consideration.

FORMAT: WHAT SHOULD YOUR RESUME LOOK LIKE?

All resumes look alike in only one respect: the applicant's name, address, and phone number are at the top. That's it! The remainder of the resume is for you to design according to the type of format you select for your purposes. Even after you have chosen a format, there is still room to arrange information in various ways for the proper emphasis that *you* want to give it. As you read through the resume samples in this book, you will see different layout designs that look attractive and are easy to read. Select the one that allows you to arrange your personal information in the most easy-to-read format, highlighting the qualifications you want to emphasize.

Here are some guidelines to help you design the proper ''look'' for your resume.

1. Have substantial margins on each side of the page and at the top and bottom.
2. Single space *within* blocks of information.
3. Double space *between* blocks of information and triple space between significant *sections* of the resume.
4. Headline or highlight key phrases or sections by using capital letters, underlining, or ''bulleting'' them with a dash or asterisk. Avoid too much emphasis, however, or the important points will get lost.
5. Achieve consistency by having similar types of information in similar places on the page, e.g., dates, names, employers, positions, skill categories.
6. Periods should be used at the end of complete sentences and may be used to conclude blocks of information.
7. Use semicolons within paragraphs or information blocks to separate descriptive phrases that are not complete sentences.
8. A one-page resume is best for most people, especially first- and second-job-seekers. Exceptions to this one-page rule are people with a long work history, often fifteen years or more, with several companies and with numerous positions. Also, professionals with lists of publications, consulting jobs, public appearances, etc., may want to attach these on another page as an addendum.
9. Have someone check your final typed copy for misspelled words and typing errors.
10. Use white or lightly tinted paper in conservative colors (buff, manila, brown, beige). The envelope should match in weight and color. Keep it simple, clean, and neat. Do not use fancy, cute, or provocative folders, binders, or decorative stationery. This is not an invitation to a party. It's business.
11. Use 8½ x 11 inch paper, 20 lb. weight at the least, 60 lb. weight at the most.

VOCABULARY AND STYLE

Writing a resume is not like writing a letter, keeping a journal, or making a grocery list. There are certain *kinds of words* and *ways to phrase ideas* that are the standard jargon of a resume. But there is no ''official'' resume style. There are several styles, and the best resumes employ the stylistic tricks that say what you want to say in the best possible way.

Here are some guidelines that will make ''wording'' your resume easier.

Clarity: Choose words and phrases that are crystal clear about what you have done or what skills you have. What *you* say will always be clear *to you*. But maybe not to an employer. After you have drafted your resume (before you type it up), have someone else read it and point out any statements that are not clear or do not make sense. Then correct them—the statements, not the reader who criticized them!

Tone: Be positive and upbeat in what you say. Use dynamic action words whenever possible. If your resume sounds dull, it probably is dull. Try to locate the dull words and replace them with more exciting synonyms. For example, the dull word is often your choice of verb. It is more interesting to say ''designed a new brochure'' than ''put together'' or ''drew up'' a new brochure. ''Streamlined the filing system'' is more specific and important sounding than ''changed the filing system'' or ''suggested new filing system.'' A typical phrase that is easy to overuse in a resume (and is not really very descriptive at all) is ''worked on.'' State precisely what the ''work'' was: for example, ''tested,'' ''evaluated,'' ''eliminated,'' ''distributed,'' ''arranged,'' ''improved.''

Here is a list of the more common action verbs used to describe types of work. Read through it and choose the ones that best explain what your duties were in a given job.

advised
created
managed
revised
supervised
wrote
researched
contracted
organized
designed
employed
directed
taught
operated
handled
regulated
conducted
prescribed
refined
headed
superintended
administered
presided over
advanced
audited
recommended
oversaw
completed
formed
solved
accomplished
achieved
served
helped
assisted
developed

planned
arranged
forecasted
charted
outlined
described
defined
projected
relieved
replaced
maintained
promoted
produced
established
founded
instituted
contributed
generated
originated
authored
determined
trained
improved
perfected
invented
installed
built
prepared
composed
constructed
distributed
analyzed
demonstrated
eliminated
reported

Consistency: When listing a number of duties you performed or skills you possess, be consistent in the way you word them. For instance, if you use verbs, stay with verbs; if you use nouns, stay with nouns. Try not to mix them. For example, "organized . . .," "directed . . .," "wrote . . .," "created . . ." is more consistent than to say "organized . . .," "director of . . .," "wrote . . .," "creator of . . ." However, this is not a hard and fast rule. It's better to be inconsistent, if consistency produces clumsy phrasing or awkwardness that could be misunderstood—or if consistency requires wordiness.

Brevity: Be brief. Say what you have to say in as few words as possible. *Remember that a one-page resume is the goal.* If you are like most people, you will probably find that you have written too much on your first draft and you'll have to edit your resume down to fit one page.

Performance, Not Personality: The content of what you write on a resume should concern your past performance, not your personality. Put the emphasis on deeds, duties, responsibilities—things you have done and things you can do, rather than on personality traits. It is better, for example, to state you "successfully supervised a staff of twenty" than to refer to yourself as a "top-notch, enthusiastic, easygoing supervisor." Or if you are "dedicated" and "loyal," let these personal characteristics come out in statements about the work you did, such as "consistently increased sales volume on a yearly basis."

In short, choose words and phrases that describe what you have *done* and what you *can do* for an employer. Emphasize those things that are important to your new employer, e.g., sales volume, accounts, number of people you supervised, interpersonal skills you possess. Again be positive. List the achievements and results that occurred because *you* held a particular job. Do not underestimate or undervalue the contributions you made to former employers.

I? Me? He? She?: Don't use the third person and talk about yourself as "he" or "she." It gives the impression that someone else has written your resume. On the other hand, you should not use "I" either! So what's left? Me? No!

The acceptable resume style is to avoid using "I" whenever possible. Since the entire resume is about you, it becomes redundant, egotistical sounding, and just plain boring to see every sentence contain an "I." As you will note in the sample resumes, the accepted stylistic device is to omit "I's" as subjects of sentences. "I developed a new filing system" should be shortened to "Developed new filing system." Leave out articles such as "a," "an," and "the" wherever they are not needed. Occasionally, however, you can and should use "I" if the sentence or phrase would sound clumsy or misleading without it.

The best thing to do regarding style and vocabulary is to read as many of the sample resumes as you need to in order to get the "feel" of how and what to say.

WHAT GOES ON A RESUME BESIDES YOUR WORK EXPERIENCE?

The answer to that question is simple: information that will indicate your qualifications for a job. But what is pertinent information? What is absolutely necessary? What is optional?

Traditional resumes used to include everything from your high-school graduation date to your race and religious background. Today's modern resume is a much more selective document. There are still essentials that must be included, but there are other pieces of information about yourself that you may or may not include.

Personal Directory

At the very top of the resume page should be your name, your mailing address, and a phone number where you can be reached. If you do not want to receive calls at your present place of employment, list only your home phone and designate it "home" or "evenings."

Job Objective

Directly beneath your name, address, and phone number should be a clear statement about your job objective, following a heading such as "Career Goal," "Job Target," "Position Desired," or simply "Job Objective."

Resumes get passed around and are often separated from cover letters. A brief clear statement of the job you seek will indicate to any reader the purpose of your resume. A clearly stated job objective is especially important if you send your resume to an employment agency where it must be filed with hundreds of others by occupation.

Some job objectives consist of one word; some are several lines. Some are deliberately vague, others deliberately specific.

Here are important options and guidelines for stating your job objective:

1. Simply state your current position or occupation, such as "Secretary," "Attorney," "Photographer," "Accountant."
2. State the general position you are seeking, especially if you are making a second job-change and expect a level higher than your current status. Examples: "Art Director," "Office Manager," "Head Teller," "Assistant Plant Manager."
3. Indicate your expectations regarding the job. "Art Director with a small or medium-sized advertising firm," "Laboratory Technician with possibility of advancement to supervisory position," "Public Relations Officer for a service organization," "Dental Hygienist requiring 25–30 hours of work per week."
4. Define your geographic limits if these are important to you. "Credit Manager for a West Coast firm," "Teaching position within the St. Louis School District." This information lets an employer with no opening at the present time know that you would be willing to take a job with other companies in the given area. If he or she knows of such an opening, your resume may get passed on to the company who might hire you.

5. State specifically the job title or work project, including the company or agency to which you are applying. "Researcher on Project 21 with Department of Human Resources," "News Announcer for Station WTCM," "Assistant Librarian in the Children's Department, Brentwood Branch."

There are several advantages and disadvantages to this approach. The advantages are: it indicates to the reader that you have prepared this resume especially for him or her and that it is *not* part of a mass mailing; it shows that you are already knowledgeable about the company and know there is an opening or an area that specifically interests you; it makes it more likely that the resume will be passed on immediately to appropriate personnel; lastly, it indicates that you consider yourself especially qualified for a position with the company and that your resume was written to clearly reflect those qualifications. In sum, it singles your resume out of dozens or hundreds of others as being especially designed and written for this particular position, company, or agency.

Some disadvantages are that you will have to type your resume for each job you apply for (with the possibility of making typos!). If you have access to a word processor, however, just alter the job goal accordingly with each resume. A specifically targeted resume makes it appear that you are interested in *only* that job or position with the company. But perhaps you are! Frequently a career-changer is more selective about the particular new job he or she is willing to give up an old career for and will apply only for jobs of particular interest that come along. A targeted resume such as this is highly recommended for such career-changers. But if you are willing to take any job or position, then leave your job objective more general so that an employer will consider you for other positions as well.

6. Some resumes, especially those in the traditional professions such as lawyers, architects, teachers, clergy, do not always need a job objective. Simply begin with your name and address, then your "professional experience" organized according to one of the three basic resume types.

Education

Your educational background must be included somewhere on your resume. Even if you have not graduated or received a degree, the years spent in study and the courses you have taken are valuable educational experience that may qualify you for a particular job. The place on the resume to position your educational data depends on several factors.

If you are a recent college graduate with little work experience, then "Education" should come early on your resume page. If it has been many years since you were in school, your education is less important than your work experience and it can be placed farther down the page. On the other hand, if you need to emphasize your educational experience (because you are a recent college graduate or you are in a field in which degrees are important), don't forget to list extracurricular subjects and activities that help qualify you for the job. Mention special honors, such as Dean's List, cum laude, scholarships, internships, etc.

If you have college degrees, it is not necessary to include your high school and graduation date. Some people do, however, as a subtle statement of where they grew up, or to let the graduation date suggest how old they are.

Education or training experiences other than traditional college courses can be important too. Special seminars, intern programs, fieldwork, workshops, in-house training programs, night or weekend courses should be included if they relate to your career or the job you seek. Indicate the certificates, diplomas, awards, or licenses received from the study. If you did not complete a program, but the number of hours or courses you took is impressive, indicate them. For example, "30 hours in business administration." In general, any career-related educational activity should be mentioned.

The format for educational data may vary, but the essential elements are: name of school, city and state, year of graduation (or years attended), degree awarded, major field of study.

Dates

On most resumes, every year of one's adult life should be accounted for, from high school or college graduation to the present. Employers look for continuity and stability in their employees. A few "missing" years may look suspicious and you may have to explain them in an interview. So however you list dates of education and employment, try to make your chronology complete. Depending on the resume format you choose, the dates will appear in either conspicuous or inconspicuous places, but they should be consistently placed on the page to make it easy for the reader to glance down them quickly to see if you have accounted for each year.

But what should you do if there are gaps in your work record?

You may have spent several years in legitimate activities that for personal reasons you do not want on a resume. For example, time recuperating from a serious illness, a year or two during which you could not find a job, time spent in a convent or monastery, a "wander year" when you just drifted to "see the world." Or perhaps the first half-dozen years after college were filled with part-time jobs while you were trying to discover your true interests and the real direction for your life. If this is your case, you should design your resume in such a way that dates are not immediately obvious to the reader. A skill-based or a functional resume can be adapted to conceal a spotty work record. (See resume samples pp. 39, 59, and 131.)

Not everyone must account for every year. Indeed, a wife or mother who has held only part-time jobs or done volunteer work over the years while she was raising children should not try to cover each year. Employers do not expect it.

In summary, if for any reason you cannot (or do not wish to) account for every year of your adult life, be sure to emphasize the skills and experiences you have had in such a way that a consistent work record is secondary to your abilities for the new job you seek.

Military Service

When two years military service was required of all American men, it was standard practice to indicate the branch of service and years spent in the military. Such is no longer the case. Therefore, it is not necessary to include military information on your resume. Do so only if it will increase your chances of getting the job; for instance, you spent extra years in the service, making it a semicareer, you had special training appropriate to the job, you learned job-related skills, you served in a country or area of the world related to the job.

Special Qualifications

Some careers demand special qualifications, such as licenses, publications, memberships in professional organizations, knowledge of foreign languages, sample work or portfolios. If any of this information is essential for your resume, highlight it (or state that it is available upon request) near the end of your resume. If it is not essential but will enhance your chances of getting the job (for instance, knowledge of a foreign language or the title of a publication in which your work has appeared), you may want to weave it into your resume under job descriptions or duties and responsibilities or skills.

Personal Information

Some years ago, every resume included certain information listed under "Personal," usually at the tail-end of a resume. It included such data as age, sex, marital status, number of children, race, ethnic background, religion, health, and hobbies. Under recent Federal and State Privacy Acts, none of this information need be offered to a potential employer, even in an interview (of course "sex" will become obvious at the interview stage if you have concealed it on your resume by using your initial rather than first name). Some state laws are even stricter than the federal law, such as New York's, which allows a job applicant to refuse information regarding previous or current psychiatric care or sexual preference.

The point is that you have the legal right to refuse this information *prior* to receiving a job. (Once hired, however, a company will need to know certain things like age, marital status, number of dependents, etc., for health insurance programs or income tax forms.) If you suspect you have been turned down for a job for refusing to answer these "personal" questions, you have legal recourse. Contact the American Civil Liberties Union for assistance.

But should you include this information on your resume?

The answer is: yes, if it will help you get the job; no, if it won't. Yes, if your resume is so short it needs a filler; no, if there isn't room. It's up to you. Here are some suggestions though.

Age: If you think you are too young or too old for a job, *don't* include your birthdate. A reader will probably "sleuth out" your age from graduation dates and years of employment, but you do not have to broadcast it on the resume. Sometimes young people in their late twenties or early thirties fear they may not be considered for an interview because of a lack of experience or because they would have to supervise much older and seasoned workers who might resent them because of their age. Leave your age off the resume, and let your potential employer decide at the interview whether your personality and experience will compensate for your youth.

The same is true if you suspect you will be considered too old. Let the interview bring out your youthful qualities and tactfully emphasize your experiences and accomplishments, indicating that they are more important than your chronological age.

Sex: Sex is hard to conceal! But the purpose of a resume is to get an interview, and if you think that your sex, announced boldly by your first name at the top of the page, might dissuade an employer from reading on and discovering your real qualifications, use your initials. Most employers today are aware of the equal opportunity laws and the training and education that many women now enjoy. But if an employer has his or her mind made up about hiring one sex over the other (and sometimes hiring committees decide this long before a job is even advertised!), you probably won't get the job no matter what you put on the resume sheet. If you think this may be the case or you are applying for a job still traditionally considered to belong to the other sex, fake it. At least on the resume.

Marital Status: There is no need to announce that you are single, married, divorced, widowed, or living with someone. (If you are a woman, you need not even enter "maiden name" on an application form.) However, if you are single and suspect that an employer might be more ready to interview a single person because the job involves travel or is low paying, state that you are. If you are married and think that being "settled and stable" is to your advantage, or you know that your interviewer places high value on family life, state that you are married and indicate the number of children you have.

Race/Ethnic Background/Religion: It is best to leave this off a resume since an employer or someone on a hiring committee may have blatant or subconscious prejudices. But again, if you know that race or religion could be to your advantage, you should indicate it indirectly by mentioning fraternal organizations, clubs, schools, or other memberships you belong to that would reveal your racial or religious heritage.

Health: It's amazing how many resume writers are in "excellent" health! As if writing resumes were an aerobic activity! Most resume readers, however, don't care if you describe yourself as "excellent," "good," "fair," or "lousy." They will probably still ask you something about the number of days you usually miss because of illness no matter what you put down.

Nevertheless, a serious question arises concerning the handicapped. A physical handicap that does not prevent you from performing the tasks required in a particular job should not prevent you from being considered for it. Here, too, if you think you have been discriminated against because of a physical handicap that is not disabling to the job, you have legal recourse. But should you indicate your handicap on a resume? No. The place to inform your employer about it is in the cover letter, and then in such a way as to let him or her know that your physical condition is not disabling for the type of work you are applying for. (See section on cover letters.)

Hobbies/Interests: The modern professional resume is an account of your work record, skills, and career accomplishments, not what you enjoy doing in your off hours. Hobbies and interests should never take up the space that could be used for important career information. Only include these if your resume is short and looks skimpy, or if your hobbies in some way make you a better candidate for the job, or you know that you share certain interests with your potential employer.

Sometimes hobbies and activities describe some aspect about yourself that you would like your potential employer to know about but could not easily work into other sections of the resume. For example, an older candidate for a job who is a marathon runner is also stating that he or she is quite healthy, maybe even healthier than younger applicants. Or people confined to wheelchairs (mentioned in the cover letter, not the resume) indicate their ability to get around town if they belong to a good number of city-wide clubs and organizations. Similarly, a very young person who has held an elective office in a civic organization is implying an ability to deal with people, win their confidence, and assume responsibility in spite of youth.

References

On most resumes, state only that "references are available on request." As with "health," employers expect your references to say "excellent" things about you, and most are not interested in hearing them until they have met you and have formulated a few specific questions of their own to ask your references. So in general, do not list them on your resume. Should an employer call a reference before seeing you, an incomplete or misinterpreted image of you might be created before you even meet your interviewer. *You* should want to make the first impression on your employer, not let someone else do it. Even an overly favorable recommendation can work against you—because you have

to live up to it and prove it in a half-hour interview or your potential employer will suspect your reference was exaggerating about your fine qualities! Another reason for not listing references is that if you send out a mass mailing of resumes, too many calls might annoy your references and they will grow less inclined to talk over the phone or give a complete picture of you.

Exceptions to this rule of not listing references: if you are seeking your first job and your resume is thin (for instance, if you are a recent college graduate or a returning housewife), you may want to list a few references both to fill up the resume page and to show your potential employer that in spite of your limited work record, there are people in the community who will vouch for your skills and qualifications. Another reason you may wish to include specific names is if they are well-known people and it would enhance your qualifications to have worked with or for them. (On the other hand, "name dropping" can also be done tactfully in the job description.)

THE TWELVE MOST COMMON RESUME FAULTS

1. Poor physical appearance due to sloppy typing, misspelled words, uneven margins, inconsistent spacing between blocks of information.
2. Disorganized so that an employer has to hunt for information.
3. Too lengthy. One page is enough.
4. Too short. Not enough information, particularly in describing what your duties were on various jobs.
5. Unnecessary information, unrelated to your job qualifications.
6. Failure to state your job objective or career goal.
7. A mere listing of positions or jobs you have held without descriptions of them.
8. Sending the wrong kind of resume for the job you seek. While it is okay to mail multiple copies of your basic resume out in a mass mailing, sometimes a resume should be rewritten and a different type or format used so that it is targeted for a specific position or company.
9. Stating your salary requirements. Most employers know that people seek new jobs to better their salaries. They also know that there are many variables in any discussion of salary: insurance benefits, company housing, transportation, health care, even a willingness to take a salary cut at the beginning because of promised promotions later, accompanied by salary raises. Say nothing about your salary until it comes up in the interview.
10. Sending a photo of yourself unless requested to do so. For one thing, it implies that you are counting on looks to get you the job and suggests that your actual credentials may be weak. For another thing, employers may form a first impression of you based on some person or some type of person you remind them of. Be aware also that if an employer requests a photo for a job that has nothing to do with personal looks (i.e., not a modeling or acting type of job), it may be a subtle form of racial or ethnic screening.
11. Dating a resume. Your resume will stay current until your job status changes unless there is a date on it; then it will look out-of-date very quickly.
12. Leaving out important directory information such as your mailing address or telephone number.

PART II

Sample Resumes That Work

INDEX BY FIELDS
OF WORK

CROSS-REFERENCE BY TYPE OF JOB-SEEKER AND TYPE OF RESUME

TYPES OF JOB-SEEKERS:
  First-job-seekers:
    Recent College Graduates: Pages 37, 43, 55, 60, 65, 74, 80, 83, 87, 99, 103, 106, 113, 120, 128, 139, 142, 150, 154, 158, 159

    Housewives/Mothers: Pages 66, 76, 124, 133, 144, 152
  Second-job-seekers:
    Pages 38, 40, 44, 49, 62, 63, 64, 68, 69, 78, 86, 90, 93, 95, 100, 102, 104, 108, 110, 112, 115, 117, 121, 126, 129, 132, 136, 137, 138, 141, 145, 147, 149, 151, 155, 157, 161
  Career-changers:
    Pages 37, 42, 45, 47, 48, 50, 52, 53, 56, 57, 67, 71, 73, 77, 81, 84, 91, 92, 94, 98, 107, 109, 111, 116, 118, 122, 123, 127, 131, 134, 140, 146, 148, 153, 156
  Job-seekers with Special Military Experience:
    Pages 47, 63, 80, 89, 92, 110, 119, 135

TYPES OF RESUMES:
  Skill-based:
    Pages 37, 38, 41, 42, 44, 45, 49, 52, 53, 55, 59, 67, 68, 70, 75, 78, 81, 84, 86, 87, 88, 90, 92, 93, 95, 97, 100, 106, 111, 112, 113, 114, 116, 119, 121, 122, 124, 126, 127, 128, 130, 132, 134, 140, 142, 144, 146, 148, 150
  Functional:
    Pages 39, 40, 43, 46, 47, 54, 57, 65, 69, 72, 74, 76, 77, 80, 89, 96, 99, 102, 105, 108, 110, 117, 118, 120, 129, 131, 135, 138, 139, 141, 145, 149, 151, 153, 155, 157, 159
  Chronological:
    Pages 58, 61, 71, 82, 85, 98, 101, 107, 125, 136, 143, 152, 160
  Combination Emphasis:
    Pages 48, 50, 51, 56, 60, 62, 63, 64, 66, 73, 79, 83, 91, 94, 103, 104, 109, 115, 123, 133, 137, 147, 154, 156, 158, 161

Accountant
Recent college graduate and career-changer
Type of resume: **skill-based**
Special circumstances: a career changer who went back to college for a Master's degree while working in a bank; job objective purposely open-ended to allow for a higher entry position because of degree.

Gerald Powell
267 Oaklawn Drive
Omaha, Nebraska 68119
(402) 354-9385

Objective: a challenging position in an accounting department of a large company that will provide opportunity for growth and professional development

Education: M.B.A., Accounting Concentration, Creighton University, Omaha, 1983
B.A. in Political Science, Desmet College, Omaha, 1977

Areas of Study:

Basic, Intermediate, and Advanced Accounting
Cost Accounting
Planning and Control
Tax Law
Business Law
Investments
Statistical Methods
Business Mathematics

Master's Thesis: "Systems and Procedures for Auditing the Medium-Large Nonprofit Firm"

Work Experience:

State Bank of Omaha
—Payroll Teller
—facilitated transactions with payroll personnel of various companies and organizations that were customers of the bank regarding distribution of employee checks
(1977-present)

—Teller
—received deposits and paid out withdrawals
(1975-1976)

Sears and Company, Omaha
—Salesclerk and cashier
—demonstrated and sold home appliances
(1973-1975)

References available on request.

Accountant with public accounting firm
Second-job-seeker
Type of resume: **skill-based**

Beverly Raferty
2830 Sprucedale Lane
Oklahoma City, OK 73102
(405) 394-5926

Career Goal

position in accounting/finance
with management possibilities

Skills

* handle general cost accounting procedures

* prepare balance sheets to reflect client's
  assets, liabilities, and capital

* audit contracts, orders, and vouchers

* record disbursements, expenses, and tax payments

* assist in designing systems for budget and cash flow forecasting

* handle industrial, financial, brokerage, and insurance accounting

Employer

Gross, Hammerman, and Associates
Oklahoma City, Oklahoma (1979-present)

Education

B.A. in Accounting, University of Oklahoma,
Stillwater, Oklahoma, 1979
C.P.A. 1979

References

available on request

Accounting Clerk
Job-changer
Type of resume: **functional**
Special circumstances: a spotty work record; dates of
employment and unemployment not emphasized; a drifter or
wanderer over the ten years since graduating from college; spent
youth engaged in hiking and camping as indicated in "hobbies."

Randolph Bettersly
3958 Maple Ave.
Boston, MA 02184
(617) 450-9385 (evenings)

Job Goal: Accounting Clerk

Work Experience

Cash Accounting Clerk, Cape Marine Supplies, Boston
—prepared journal entries; checked accounting records for completeness and
accuracy; verified data and reconciled any discrepancies (1981-present).

Night Auditor, The Oasis Club, Charleston, West Virginia
—audited customer receipts; read out cash registers and balanced sales; prepared
daily business report (1979).

Assistant Manager/Accounts Payable, Blue Grass Distributors, Louisville, Kentucky
—hired as accounts payable clerk (1975-1976); promoted to assistant manager;
supervised 12 people; processed approximately 300 invoices daily (1976).

Accounting Clerk Trainee, Sanders Foods, Lexington, Kentucky
—prepared vouchers; entered postings, maintained records; wrote reports and
summaries (1973-1974).

Education

B.A. in Business/Accounting, Frankfort College, Frankfort, Kentucky, 1973.

Personal

Date of birth: August 30, 1952
Single
Health: excellent
Hobbies: have backpacked Continental Divide and Appalachian Trails; sailing, mountain
climbing.

Willing to relocate

Auditor
Second-job-seeker
Type of resume: **functional**

George Zink
2938 Michigan Ave. Apt 369
Chicago, Illinois 60613
(312) 394-5828

Job Objective: Director of Internal Auditing

Director of Internal Auditing

—supervised and managed staff of ten; responsible for all corporate accounting functions;
statements, cost accountings, payroll, inventory control, data processing reports;
inspected journal and ledger entries to determine that proper recording procedures
were followed; implemented improved inventory and payroll systems; revised billing
system which resulted in annual savings of $40,000; prepared status reports for
financial board (1975-present).

Senior Internal Auditor

—responsible for examination of accounting records; preparation of financial reports;
verification of ledger entries of purchases, expenses, payments; supervised and trained
junior auditors (1971-1975).

Internal Auditor Trainee

—a two-year training program after which I was promoted to junior auditor
(1968-1971).

Employer: Lakeshore Caterers, Chicago, Illinois

Education: B.A. in Accounting, De Paul University, Chicago, 1968

C.P.A. 1970

Personal: Birthdate 8/3/48
Married, two children
Health excellent

Willing to relocate outside Chicago area.

References available on request.

Sam O'Brien
4928 Deerpark Road
Clayton, MO 63116
(314) 394-5820

Career Goal: Controller/Treasurer

Areas of Expertise:

Controllership   Payroll
Corporate Accounting   Taxes
Industrial Accounting   Budgets
Cost Accounting   Forecasts
Auditing   Financial Statements
Inventory Control   Supervision

Achievements:

* reduced period-end financial reporting by three days
* reduced accounts receivable by $65,000
* designed cost reduction program that saved $85,000 annually
* lowered expenditures for outside CPA firm from $15,000 to $10,000 with improved
  internal auditing controls
* responsible for all accounting operations during major plant expansion program

Work History:

1975-present   Controller/Treasurer
                    Meramec Earthworks, Inc., Clayton, MO

1967-1975   Chief Cost Accountant/Controller
                    Gravois Slab and Tile Company, St. Louis, MO

1961-1967   Senior Accountant
                    Frederick Lindenbush and Company, C.P.A.
                    St. Louis, MO

Education:

1961   B.A. in Accounting, University of Illinois, Edwardsville
       Member: C.P.A. Association of Missouri

Assistant Account Executive with an advertising company
Career-changer
Type of resume: **skill-based**
Special circumstances: after a long career in advertising for various businesses, Fred is seeking a job in an advertising firm.

Fred Thompson
5990 Lucas Blvd. Apt. 30-D
Columbus, Ohio 43214
(614) 778-3406

Job Target: Assistant Account Executive

Capabilities:

* coordinate sales promotion activities
* research product and potential market for most successful ad campaigns
* coordinate media planning; buy media time
* prepare materials and conduct sales meetings
* devise marketing strategy in consultation with sales departments
* review bids and contract out facets of production
* write original copy
* supervise artwork, layout, and production
* possess technical knowledge of most major reproduction processes
* write and distribute public relations releases
* supervise trade shows and national press shows
* supervise and distribute in-house news releases
* act as liaison and coordinator of services with outside advertising agencies

Work Experience:

Coordinator of Advertising and Promotion
Bissell Furniture, Columbus, OH (1978-present)

Assistant Advertising Coordinator
Hinkley Department Store, Chicago, IL (1972-1978)

Associate Advertising Sales Manager
Audubon Life Monthly, Chicago, IL (1970-1972)

Salesman
Ralston Purina, St. Louis, MO (1966-1968)

Education:

1970   Associates Certificate, Randolph Quincy School of Advertising, Chicago, IL
1966   B.A. in Business and Psychology, University of Missouri, St. Louis

References available upon request.

Willing to relocate outside the Midwest.

Advertising Assistant
First-job-seeker/recent college graduate
Type of resume: **functional**

John Anders
2418 Cascade Ave.
Seattle, WA 98112
(206) 378-3399

Objective: Entry position as advertising assistant

Education: B.A. in Communications, Portland University, 1982
               Major Fields: advertising, marketing, psychology, journalism, consumer behavior,
                   graphic arts

Experience:

        Advertising Intern, Marketing Showplace, Seattle, Summer 1981

        Handling and servicing five accounts for advertising director; duties included
        designing and laying out ads in coupon format, writing copy, and working in
        traffic control.

        Advertising Clerk, Oregon City Gazette, part-time, 1979-1981

        Measured and drew dummy ads for newspaper copy; computed total inches of
        news and ads; estimated total number of newspaper pages needed for next day's
        edition; translated data from dummy copy to production work-sheets and
        delivered to appropriate departments for review.

        Reporter, Oregon City Gazette, free-lance, 1978-82

        Wrote feature articles on conservation and wildlife; covered Environmental
        Protection Agency conferences; also took and developed photos for wildlife
        illustrations to accompany articles.

        Stencil Designer, Cascade Chapter, Sierra Club, 1980

        Designed stencils for chapter newsletter; wrote copy.

References available upon request.

Willing to relocate; prefer West Coast.

Copywriter
Second-job-seeker
Type of resume: **skill-based**

Myra Hopkins
435 East 53rd Street Apt. 28-B
New York, NY 10034
(212) 454-8979

Career Goal: Copywriter for advertising agency

Skills:

RESEARCH
—carry out product research
—create consumer profile studies
—research competitor products and advertising strategies
—perform tasks assigned by copy chief and account executives
—can consistently meet deadlines

WRITING
—write copy for specifically targeted audiences: housewives, high-school students,
 professionals
—adapt data and copy to specialized formats: full-page ads, slogans, captions for photos
 or illustrations, jingles
—produce extended copy for full-length articles appearing in one monthly brochure and
 two quarterly newsletters

PRODUCT KNOWLEDGE
—clothing, toiletries, cosmetics, luggage, personal office/desk equipment, travel programs

Present Employer:

Marvin Drew and Associates, NYC, 1979-present

Education:

B.A. in Philosophy, Bennington College, VT, 1979
Cum laude

Writing Samples available upon request

Advertising Media Planner
Career-changer
Type of resume: **skill-based**
Special circumstances: after long experience as a media buyer
and media planner for advertising agencies, Gail is seeking a
career in television; her dual job objective suggests her
willingness to take any position in an area in which she is
qualified.

Gail Kelly
2491 Myrlette Court
Kansas City, MO 64112
(913) 304-5923

JOB TARGET: Production assistant or promotion director with local TV station

Video Production   casting; script writing; audio selection and placement; lighting design;
                      camera angles, shooting procedures, editing; voice-overs; slide and
                      cue-card production; research topics and determine best production values
                      for marketing accounts; create mock-up presentation for planning and
                      selection stages of promotion.

Media Planning   analyze marketing objectives; consult with clients regarding best media
                      strategies; create budget for media campaign; research television usage of
                      spot commercials and evaluate their results; negotiate air-time rates for
                      client-customers.

Promotion   organize creatively and write promotional pieces; evaluate content and
                      theme in terms of desired effect; cut and splice audio and video tapes to
                      meet established air length; consult with and advise clients on
                      promotional pieces.

Work History   Gage, Darnell, and Warren Inc., Kansas City
                          Media Planner, 1974 to present

                      Halbrand and Wolf, Inc., Kansas City
                          Assistant Media Planner, 1971-1974
                          Media Buyer, 1969-1971

Education   B.S. in Business, Arkansas State University,
                          Fayetteville, AR, 1968
                      —course of studies concentration in marketing and advertising

References available upon request.

Assistant Production Manager/Traffic Manager in advertising
Job-changer
Type of resume: **functional**
Special circumstances: Lorna is seeking her second job in an
advertising company; present employer omitted from resume
to prevent them from learning of her job search through the
professional ''grapevine.''

Lorna C. Sultana
2316 84th Street
Brooklyn, NY 11214
(212) 938-7492 Evenings

Job Objective: Assistant Production Manager or Traffic Manager

1979-Present   Assistant Production Manager

          —Supervise production and printing of major national publication; buy all separations for the monthly Product Mover; heavy client and agency contact; coordinate all art and mechanicals and final films with stripping department; in-depth media background-contact with newspapers across country; copywriting for trade sell sheets.

1976-1979   Assistant to Promotion Director
          Kings Plaza Shopping Center and Marina
          Brooklyn, NY

          —Originally hired as gal friday to handle typing, bookkeeping, media contracts, schedules; promoted to assistant to promotion director; responsibilities included conducting all shopping-center promotions and events; placing of advertising and publicity in and out of shopping center; preparing presentations for special interest groups; arranging photography for VIP visitors and bookings of the Community Room.

Education: 1975 B.S. in Marketing, Brooklyn College, NY

          1971 Science Diploma, Whitman High School, Huntington, Long Island

Personal: Born January 30, 1954
          Single
          Health excellent

Willing to relocate.

References available upon request.

Ralph Esposito
4820 Bandler Road
Miami, Florida 33167
(305) 495-2847

Objective: Aircraft Inspector for Federal Aviation Administration

Summary: 22 years as aircraft mechanic and aircraft maintenance supervisor

Airplane Mechanics: experienced in preventive engine maintenance (replacement of spark
      plugs, oil changes, lube jobs, general tune-ups); can locate and repair airframe
      deterioration; tighten airframe; make equipment repairs and inspections according
      to specifications; coordinate refueling operations; supervise complete FAA
      inspections and write up finished reports.

Employee Supervision: have hired and trained airplane mechanics for 12 years; can
      coordinate shop work, make out time schedules, work well with shop foremen,
      handle labor-personnel disputes among workers.

Management: purchase supplies, fuel, equipment; create and work within budget; have
      knowledge of shop layout for optimal work flow.

Work Experience:

      Pan American Airways, Miami, Florida

      Chief Maintenance Supervisor, 1978-present
      Assistant Maintenance Supervisor, 1970-1978
      Aircraft Mechanic, 1962-1970

      Pompano Airways, Fort Lauderdale, Florida

      Aircraft Mechanic, 1960-1962

Military: U.S. Army 1955-1960
      —assigned to aircraft maintenance

Education: Lauderdale Technical High School 1951-1955

Personal: Born July 6, 1937
      Married, three children
      Health excellent

Francine Delancey
4958 Macon Ave.
Atlanta, Georgia 30354
(404) 495-2288

Career Objective: Position in personnel/employee relations with an international airline

Work Experience:

Delta Airlines, Corporate Headquarters, Atlanta, GA

Training Supervisor (1978-present)

—assisted instructional staff in training programs for flight attendants; initiated
new training programs; conducted career workshops in Atlanta area colleges and
high schools; conducted personal appearance seminars (uniforms, grooming,
speech, body language) for small groups of flight attendants, ticket clerks,
porters; requested by Delta to further education at company's expense in areas
of group dynamics, psychology, interpersonal communications.

Flight Attendant (1975-1978)

—after completing Delta's training program, began as junior flight attendant;
promoted to senior flight attendant for domestic and international flights.

Education:

Davis Community College, Atlanta
—night courses and weekend workshops in psychology and interpersonal
communications; total hours 50

Decatur University, Atlanta
—B.A. in Theater Arts (1974)

Personal: Born 1954, Macon, Georgia
Single
Hobbies: theater, movies, reading, travel

References available upon request.

Commercial Pilot
Second-job-seeker
Type of resume: **skill-based**
Special circumstances: William graduated from college in 1967
but did not go into aviation until 1978; jobs held between these
years are omitted because not related to job objective.

William Geltzman
3999 Navaho Lane Apt. 3
Phoenix, AZ 85021
(602) 440-3967

OCCUPATION: Commercial Pilot

EXPERIENCE: —Command crew, passengers, and craft
—Fly 747 jets, running at speeds approaching sound
—Handle night and instrument flying
—Pilot international and overseas flights
—Transport passengers, mail, freight
—Recognize adverse weather and ground conditions
—Handle all aspects of flight plans including ship's papers regarding fuel
  supply, weight, etc.
—Understand all electronic and mechanical systems of craft
—Can certify worthiness of craft by inspecting airframe, operating
  equipment, engines

LICENSES: Flight Engineer License: 26-432-81-OH
Commercial Pilot License: JH-321-498
Radio Telephone Operator Permit: B27-45-IH2

MEMBERSHIPS: Airline Pilots Association, Washington, D.C.
Association of Commercial Aviators, Chicago, IL

EDUCATION: 1979 Flying Diploma, Phoenix Aviation School, Phoenix, AZ
1967 B.S. in Mechanical Engineering, University of Arizona, Phoenix

EMPLOYMENT: 1980-present Commercial Pilot, Trans World Airlines
1978-1980 Flight Engineer, American Airlines

References available upon request.

Susan Osburn
2475 Stanford Street
Chicago, Illinois 60632
(312) 450-3558 (Evenings)

OBJECTIVE:	To work for a major airline company in either advertising or promotion department
1976-present	<u>Assistant Director for Sales and Development</u> Empire Travel Sales, Corporate Headquarters, Chicago Researched conference facilities nationwide for advertising in trade publications and journals; applied readership data (profile, demographics, subscriptions) to determine best advertising strategy and to select best vehicles for promotion; devised, implemented, and evaluated advertising campaigns; created unique and individual presentations for conference planning; wrote copy for ads aimed at individuals and groups; researched international operational costs; prepared budget for each advertising program.
1974-1976	<u>Branch Manager</u> A-1 Travel, Chicago Supervised a staff of 12 in this local branch of Empire Travel; specialized in programs for executive travel; catered to civic and fraternal organizations; in first year reduced operational costs by 25 percent and increased sales volume by 10 percent.
1972-1974	<u>Ticket Agent</u> Made general domestic and international travel and hotel reservations; booked flights, train reservations, hotel and resort accommodations; eventually specialized in international reservations due to my travel experience in 28 foreign countries (Europe, Central and South America, Africa) and fluent knowledge of Spanish, French, German.
1970-1972	<u>Airline Reservationist</u> Pan American Airways, Chicago Made domestic and international flight reservations; learned use of teletype and small computer terminals.
Education:	B.A. Mundelein College, Chicago; majored in Comparative Literature; lived and studied in Frankfort, Germany, during junior year.

Architect
Job-changer
Type of resume: **chronological with functional emphasis**

John R. Ferguson
2439 Deneb Drive
Charlotte, North Carolina 27613
(704) 382-7791

JOB OBJECTIVE: Position with Architectural Restorations, Inc., St. Louis, Missouri

PROFESSIONAL EXPERIENCE

1977-Present   King Mills Architectural Associates, Charleston, S.C.

                 Junior Partner
                 Analyzed and recommended site selections; assisted in feasibility studies,
                 including cost analysis; presented master plans to board of directors for
                 approval; drew up final plans for clients; under supervision of senior
                 partner, presented final plans to clients; acted as liaison with municipal
                 boards responsible for approving building plans; projects included Front
                 Street Mall, Charleston, and Beaufort Plaza, Beaufort, S.C.

1970-1977   Eaves and Whiteside, Inc., Charlotte, N.C.

                 Specifications Writer
                 Rendered directions and explanations of architectural plans for use by
                 contractors and other on-site building personnel; prepared program
                 development reports regarding cost analysis and building code analysis;
                 assisted with interior design proposals for Catholic Charity Project of
                 rehabilitating low-cost housing for senior citizens.

1965-1967   Blackwell Architects, Charlotte, N.C.

                 Draftsman
                 Created models and architectural drawings for in-house use; also
                 researched applications for federal grants; made final sketches
                 accompanied by notes and specified dimensions.

EDUCATION

1971   M.A., Washington University School of Architecture, St. Louis, Missouri
                 Internship with Howdershell Planners, St. Charles, Missouri
1965   B.A., University of South Carolina, mechanical engineering
1961   Roanoke High School, Fleasburg, S.C.

Licensed: States of North Carolina, South Carolina, Missouri
Memberships: American Association of Architects
                 Appointed to Landmarks Historical Association, Charleston, 1975;
                 Chairman, Preservation Advisory Board, 1980-1982.

Roger Bancroft
317 East 86th Street Apt. 30-G
New York, New York 10013
(212) 676-3648 (evenings)

Career Target: Managerial position with the New York City
                  Department of Building Inspectors

SKILLS/KNOWLEDGE:

* Design engineering
* Cost estimates
* Specification writing
* Preparation of design criteria
* Supervision of drawings
* Building codes
* Supervision of field site visits
* Coordination of other engineering groups

AREAS:

* Floor systems
* Foundations
* Superstructures
* Air intake ducts
* Compressor buildings

PROJECTS:

* Vancouver University Library, Vancouver, WA
* Baton Rouge Airport, Baton Rouge, LA
* Darcy General Hospital, Denver, CO
* Union Station Renovation, St. Louis, MO

EMPLOYERS:

* 1970-present   Warner and Walsh, Inc., New York City
* 1964-1967   Holmes Engineering, Inc., Vancouver, WA

EDUCATION:

* B.S. in Civil Engineering, Cornell University, 1964
* M.A. in Industrial Engineering, Stanford University, 1970

Landscape Architect/Botanist
Career-changer
Type of resume: **skill-based**
Special circumstances: after being trained and having worked several
years as a landscape engineer, Pam decided to return to the type of
work she did as an intern in a state botanical garden.

PAM DUNCAN   14 Donelson Pike   Nashville, TN 37213   (615) 459-3395

Objective: Assistant Director of a state botanical garden

BOTANY

* Determine maximal land use in terms of existing environment (sunlight, temperature, soil conditions, surrounding flora, drainage, etc.)
* Provide for optimum health of plants and future growth
* Distribute floral clusters and shade tree groupings to enhance aesthetic quality of landscape
* Provide optional listings of trees, shrubs, plants, flowers appropriate to given ecological conditions

ARCHITECTURAL DESIGN

* Develop initial plans for exterior renovation and landscape engineering
* Recommend master design in harmony with surrounding buildings and natural phenomena
* Determine institution's space needs and program development
* Render maps showing land elevations and existing buildings, roads, natural phenomena

PROJECT MANAGEMENT

* Supervise all stages of projects from early feasibility studies to completion
* Act as liaison with building architects and road engineers
* Represent architectural firm/agency to client and government board of supervisors

FUNDING

* Draw up grant applications for local, state, and federal funding
* Establish budgets and work within them
* Determine cost analysis and estimates for supplies and labor

WORK EXPERIENCE

1978-present   Junior Landscape Engineer, Tennessee State Park Commission, Nashville
1974-1978   Design Supervisor, Cumberland Renovations, Inc., Nashville
1973-1974   Intern, Knoxville Botanical Gardens, Knoxville

EDUCATION: B.A. in botany and landscape engineering (double major), University of Tennessee, Knoxville, 1974
Licensed: State of Tennessee
Member: American Association of Landscape Architects

Commercial Artist/Art Director with advertising agency
Job-changer
Type of resume: **functional**

Janet Pisano
238 West 10th St.
New York, NY 10005
(212) 858-7734

Career Goal: Art Director with a large advertising agency in New York area

Professional Experience

SENIOR ART DIRECTOR
    —hired among the first team of artists for this new company, I was promoted to Art
    Director after two years. Supervised creative staff; in charge of all art work; responsible
    for hiring artists, researchers, copywriters, and other creative assistants. Conferred
    with clients regarding their product and possible advertising approaches; collected
    background data on product for art staff; formulated design concept. Assigned phases
    of production to artists, photographers, writers. (1976-present)

FREELANCE COMMERCIAL ARTIST
    —general boardwork, illustrations, paste-ups, mechanicals for small trade-book
    publisher and several ad agencies. (1974-1976)

RESEARCHER/COPYWRITER
    —researched market for products; made comparison studies with competitors; evaluated
    and generated advertising ideas; wrote copy for ads, flyers, easel sales presentations.
    (1973-1974)

Employers
    1976-1982   Dickson Brothers and Company, New York, NY
    1974-1976   Tuliphill Press, New York, NY
                       Riverside Advertising Corporation, Newark, NJ
                       Malco Advertising Agency, New York, NY
                       Future Ads Incorporated, New York, NY
    1973-1974   Balmer Incorporated, Chicago, IL

Education
    B.A. in Fine Arts, Princeton University, 1973
    Catskill School of Design, Binghamton, NY, Summer 1973
    Art Institute of San Francisco, San Francisco, CA,
        Summer Scholarship, 1972

Commercial Artist
First-job-seeker/recent college graduate
Type of resume: **skill-based**

Dan Anderson
2381 Maple Drive
Pittsburgh, PA 65240
(412) 231-8019

Objective: Artist in small advertising agency where there would be a wide variety of
challenging projects

SKILLS:

Illustration: accomplished in line drawing for magazine ads, slides, and
promotional materials; watercolors, acrylics

Design: experienced in all aspects of production from layout to finish, general
boardwork, paste-ups, reproductions

Photography: three years of photo journalism experience for university
newspaper and yearbook

EXPERIENCE:

Paste-up artist, New Woman magazine, New York, NY, summers 1980-present

Designer, University Yearbook, Pittsburgh University, 1981

Photographer, The University News, Pittsburgh University, 1978-present

Art Instructor, Shady Valley Camp, Blattsville, CT, summers 1978-1979

EDUCATION:

B.A. in Commercial Art, Pittsburgh University, Pittsburgh, PA, 1983

Rocky Mountain Art Institute, Boulder, CO, summer 1978

Workshop in copywriting and magazine illustrations at Pennsylvania Art Academy,
Pittsburgh, PA, 1980

References and sample work available on request.

Commercial Artist
Career-changer
Type of resume: **combination skill-based and functional**
Special circumstances: having heard of the opening with the
Sun Times and not wishing to relinquish his present job teaching,
Eric has targeted his resume very narrowly in terms of employer.

Eric Villeau
2809 Sunrise Blvd.
Phoenix, AZ 85028
(602) 882-9572

Job Target: Art Department Associate with the <u>Phoenix Sun Times</u> with possibility of
promotion to media supervisor

Skills:

illustration, layout, paste-up, research, copywriting, principles of advertising, photography

Experienced as:

* free-lance illustrator for Parker Advertising Co., Phoenix, AZ

* artistic consultant for Alumni Productions, Arizona State University

* instructor in commercial art at Camelback Mountain Community College (courses
included principles and technique of layout, paste-up, line drawing, wash, advertising,
photography, slide production, the use of drafting instruments such as brush and pen)

* designer, illustrator, and copywriter for three area educational organizations

* moderator of campus newspaper at CMCC

* creator of award-winning lobby display for Valley Bank and Trust, Scottsdale Branch

Education:

M.A. in Fine Arts, Washington University, St. Louis, MO, 1976
B.A. in Studio Art, Loretto College, St. Louis, MO, 1968

Present Employer:

Camelback Community College, Scottsdale, AZ
—instructor, 1976-present

Robert Teasdale
5938 Wausau Ave. Apt. 3-F
Elmhurst, Illinois 60613
(312) 359-3396

OBJECTIVE: Supervisory position in credit department of Diner's Club International

WORK HISTORY

Assistant Loan Officer, Oak Park Savings Bank, Chicago (1979-present)

—Supervised ten personnel in loan department
—Met with potential customers
—Originated residential and commercial real estate loans
—Evaluated all loan applications
—Made recommendations to chief loan officer
—Chaired loan review board
—Increased mortgage portfolios from 50 million to 57 million

Junior Loan Officer, Oak Park Savings Bank (1977-1979)

—Assisted customers in completing loan applications
—Checked credit references
—Made recommendations to loan approval board

Assistant Credit Accountant, Wheaton National Bank, Wheaton, IL (1974-1977)

—Began as loan approval trainee
—Appointed assistant credit accountant one year later
—Assisted loan review supervisor in credit appraisals, commercial papers,
    insolvencies

EDUCATION

1974   B.S. in Accounting, Loyola University, Chicago
1977   Credit Management Workshop sponsored by Chicago National Trust at
       University of Chicago

PERSONAL

Birthdate: April 6, 1953
Married

References available on request.

Bank Officer
Job-changer
Type of resume: **chronological**
Special circumstances: only most recent job is explained in detail
since previous positions are self-explanatory.

James R. Russell
8394 Wellington Ave.
Pittsburgh, PA 15213
(412) 839-5592

Career Goal: Vice-president of Operations

Work History

1971-present   First National Bank of Pittsburgh, Main Branch
                      Assistant Vice-president

                      * Report to senior vice-president

                      * Assist in establishing all operating procedures and policies

                      * Plan and supervise work procedures in line with bank policies

                      * Coordinate work flow, directly or indirectly responsible for successful
                        performance of duties by all lower bank staff personnel

                      * Have management and custody of assets, securities, records of bank

                      * Serve on interbank policy review board

                      * Approve and decline credit for consumer, real estate, and commercial loans

                      * As chief loan officer, handle outstandings of three million in commercial
                        and four million in retail installment loans

                      * Have assisted in planning of three branch locations

                      * Proficient in bank accounting and financial statement analysis

                      * Familiar with electronic data processing procedures

1968-1971   First National Bank of Pittsburgh, Clinton Branch, Clinton, PA
                      Branch Manager

1965-1968   Brentwood Bank, West Mifflin, PA
                      Head Teller

Education: Penn State, State College, PA 1962
                      B.S. in Accounting

Military: U.S. Navy, Second Lieutenant 1962-1965

Bank Teller
Job-changer
Type of resume: **skill-based**
Special circumstances: dates deemphasized to cover up a spotty
work record; cover letter should explain frequent job changes; see
cover letter, p. 168.

Marjorie Tracy
1593 Kenneth Drive
Santa Cruz, California 95011
(408) 554-2056

Position
BANK TELLER

Capsule
Five years experience in various teller positions

EXPERIENCE
* Pay out money withdrawn
* Receive deposits for checking
* Ascertain identification of customers
* Make deposits of savings
* Supervise statement mailing
* Handle transactions for customers buying securities
* Receive note payments on loans
* Process payroll checks for employees of business with
  accounts at bank
* Operate desk terminal of small computer

EMPLOYERS
Pasadena Savings and Loan, Pasadena, CA (1981-82)
First National, Santa Cruz, CA (1980)
Allied Merchants, San Diego, CA (1979-1980)
Harbor Trust, Santa Cruz, CA (1978)

EDUCATION
B.A. in Liberal Arts, Berkley University, 1974

References available on request.

Bookkeeper
First-job-seeker/recent college graduate
Type of resume: **combination skill-based and chronological**

John Travers
3954 Sunset Ave.
Carol City, Florida 33015
(305) 430-4602

Job Objective: Bookkeeping Position

Skills and Capabilities:

—maintain ledger records
—accounts payable
—accounts receivable
—payroll deductions
—budget forecasting
—typing invoices and vouchers
—preparing periodic statement reports

Work Experience:

1980-present	Bookkeeper (student-worker loan) University Bookstores University of Florida, Miami
1979-1980	Cashier Flamingo Room, Hotel Fountainbleu Miami, Florida
1978-1983 (summers)	Clerk in Business Office Coral Gables Country Club Coral Gables, Florida

Education:

B.S. in Business, University of Florida, Miami, 1983

References:

John Handle, Bookstore Manager, University of Florida
Pierre LaTournee, Hotel Fountainbleu, Miami
Jeff Peters, Business Manager, Coral Gables Country Club,
    Coral Gables, Florida

Marie Duffey
231 Wasatch Ave. Apt. 3-D
Salt Lake City, Utah 84126
(801) 456-2295

Position: Managerial position in a medium-sized accounting department

Work Record:

1972-present	Western Auto, Salt Lake City Manager: Accounts Payable and Accounts Receivable
1970-1972	Brigham Young University Assistant Manager: Business Office
1967-1970	United Color Separations Inc., Salt Lake City Billing Supervisor
1966-1967	Parawan Associates, Provo, Utah Secretary/Bookkeeper

Capabilities:

Maintain ledgers; type invoices and vouchers; prepare periodic financial statements; assist with internal auditing; make payroll deductions; handle accounts payable and receivable; supervise bookkeeping staff of 5 to 15 people; operate most standard office business machines

Education:

1958, Provo High School, Provo, Utah
Business Studies Diploma

Personal:

Age: 40
Married, three children

Electronics Engineer/Communications Technician
Second-job-seeker
Type of resume: **chronological with functional emphasis**

Erica York
5537 Tylersville Rd.
Dayton, OH 45416
(513) 546-2295

Career Goal: Electronics Engineer/Communications Technician

Work Experience:

Roman Electronics Systems, Inc., Dayton, OH (1979-present)

Position: technical staff engineer

Responsibilities and Achievements:

* researched special projects dealing with alternative systems integration technique

* executed on-the-spot modification of equipment

* improved processing and routing of calls through careful monitoring of traffic loads and computer simulation

* developed real-time procedures for network control

* designed preventive maintenance tests for radio receiver station

* trained 8 radio repair persons

Education:

B.S. in Electrical Engineering, Xavier University, Cincinnati, 1979
Honors: magna cum laude
Senior Seminar Project: "Cable TV Linkage for East Cincinnati: Problems and Possibilities"

Licenses:

First Class Radio Telephone
Amateur Radio

Communications Technician/Telephone Repairman
Second-job-seeker
Type of resume: **chronological with functional emphasis**
Special circumstances: job objective targeted for a specific job
opening. See cover letter page 172.

Lowell Sweeney
478 Delta Ave.
Hattiesburg, MS 39416
(601) 560-3355

Objective: Communications Technician with Gulf Coast Telephone Laboratories

Experience:

   Mississippi Consolidated Utilities, Hattiesburg

      Position: PBX Installer
               —installed and maintained PBX systems for subscribers; located and
                  rectified communications problems; reported on subscriber needs to
                  company consultants   (1979-present)

   United States Air Force, Sherman AFB, Gainesville, FL

      Position: Senior Level Radio Repairman
               —provided upkeep for radio receivers and aircraft control tower equipment;
                  installed and serviced new consoles for expanded aircraft facilities;
                  trained junior repair personnel   (1975-1979)

Education:

      Hattiesburg Community College, 1981
         —Communications Theory and Practice I and II

      Mississippi Bell Vocational Training Institute, 1980
         —PBX and CENTREX systems

      USAF Training Institute, Gainesville, FL, 1975-1976
         —Ground radio communications
         —Electronics, transistors

      Jackson High School, Jackson, MS, 1974
         —Major: calculus and physics

References available upon request.

Engineering Technician/Cameraman
Second-job-seeker
Type of resume: **skill-based and chronological combination**
Special circumstances: Brad included his college internship
program and his campus DJ job as valid work experience in
his field.

Brad Newburg
3650 Wheatley Street
Minneapolis, MI 55428
(612) 546-3396

POSITION: Engineering Technician

SKILLS:

* all camera operations for film and videotape productions

* audio-video switching

* studio lighting

* mixing

* gaffing

* set design

* script writing

* trailer narration

* dubbing

* film editing

WORK EXPERIENCE:

WMIN-TV, Minneapolis, 1979-present
—engineering assistant for evening news and special documentaries

Faroh Productions, Inc., Minneapolis, 1978
—assistant cameraman on children's life science series (college internship
  program)

QUET, Marquette University, Milwaukee, WI, 1976-1978
—engineer and disc jockey for campus radio station

EDUCATION:

B.A. in Communication Arts, Marquette University, Milwaukee, WI, 1978

Community Services
Assistant Director: Day-Care Center
First-job-seeker/recent college graduate
Type of resume: **functional**

Sylvia Pekin
5493 Harbor Drive Apt. 3
Hartford, Connecticut 06134
(203) 563-7926

Objective: Assistant Director of a day-care center

Work Experience:

Director, Day-care Services, Windsor College (1980-83)
—set up and supervised regular day-care services for faculty with children and for special campus events such as faculty dinners, weekend seminars, evening programs, and athletic activities; interviewed, selected, and supervised student volunteers.

Volunteer Teacher four afternoons per week, Treetop Day-care Center, Hartford (1980-83)
—organized play sessions, story time, outdoor activities, snack breaks; met with parents and siblings on a regular basis to discuss child's progress; wrote up reports; trained other volunteers.

Camp Counselor, Seneca Falls Summer Camp, Seneca Falls, Vermont (1978-80)
—cabin counselor in charge of eight seven-year-old campers; planned 24-hour-a-day activities; responsible for physical health and emotional well-being of my campers.

Educational Experience:

Windsor College, Hartford, Connecticut
B.A. in Early Childhood Education, 1983
Courses included:

Psychology of Learning
Educating the Exceptional Child
Rhythm and Games
Early Childhood Problems
Contemporary Social Problems: The Family
History of Childhood in America
Early Childhood Education Seminar
The Modern Day-care Center

References:

Mary O'Daly, Treetop Care Center, Hartford, CT
Professor Lydia Mantis, Head, Dept. of Education, Windsor College, Hartford, CT

Community Services
Assistant Director: Senior Citizens' Center
First-job-seeker/housewife-mother
Type of resume: **skill-based/functional combination**

Gloria Fulton
4398 Walnut Grove
Norwood, MA 02156
(617) 567-2239

Job Target: Assistant Director of a senior citizens' center

Summary: Ten years experience as volunteer worker at Hyde Park Senior Citizens' Center, Norwood, Massachusetts, with responsibilities in program development, group organization, fund raising, and supervision.

Responsibilities and Achievements:

—organized and conducted year-round social events for regular members of center
—organized intercenter socials with other senior citizens' clubs
—booked travel arrangements for bus tours, museum days, theater parties, seasonal picnics
—organized holiday care-bundle programs (Thanksgiving, Christmas, Easter) and other fund raising/contribution drives
—directed Meals-on-Wheels program (1977-1979) providing 50 meals a day for home-bound citizens
—supervised youth volunteers for home-visiting programs
—successfully wrote grant proposals for special programs
—served as bookkeeper for center (1980)

Current Memberships:

Norwood Junior League
Hyde Estates Neighborhood Association
Norwood Biennial Crafts Fair Committee

Education:

B.A. in French, Mount Holyrood College, Springdale, Massachusetts, 1962

Personal:

Married, three children
Health good
Interests: movies, reading, home-neighborhood renovation

References available.

JACK MORE   6672 Westend Ave.   Pittsburgh, PA 15276   (412) 679-3386

Objective: Supervisory position with city youth center

Program Development:

—arranged on-going job opportunities with local businesses and community agencies for teenage boys and girls
—created and ran several Boys' Clubs athletic leagues
—organized field and wildlife outings for Boy Scout Troop 181
—served as consultant for Boy Scouts of America, West Pennsylvania Region
—as program director, assumed responsibility for all daily camping activities during six two-week camping sessions

Youth Counseling:

—interviewed delinquent boys and girls (age 14-18) and their families
—determined personality/ability/interest profiles for eventual placement in foster homes
—made periodic home evaluations and wrote detailed reports
—arranged regular check-up appointments with cases assigned to me
—acted as liaison in grievance and complaint disputes between parolees and school or employment authorities

Administration:

—supervised caseworkers assigned to families needing various social services
—established operating budgets for outreach programs such as job placement, upward bound, and summer camp scholarships
—screened, trained, and supervised student volunteers in Big Brother/Sister programs
—hired, trained, and supervised staff of 40 at summer camp

Employment Record:

1974-present   Juvenile Parole Officer, Pittsburgh Parole Board

1971-1974   Program Director, Camp Winnetonga, Alleghany National Forest,
(summers)   Sheffield, PA

1971-74   Teacher, Natrona Senior High School, Natrona, PA

Education: B.S. in Chemistry, Bradley University, Peoria, IL 1971

Memberships: American Association of Parole Officers
                Pennsylvania Correctional Association
                American Camping Association
                Boy Scouts of America

Computers
Data Processing Supervisor
Second-job-seeker
Type of resume: **skill-based**

Carl Hampton
3357 Mountain Road
Manchester, NH 03168
(603) 564-2297

Objective: Data Processing Supervisor

Equipment:

—can operate off-line data-processing equipment: sorters, interpreters, card punchers, tape duplicators, tape units on stored programs, card processors, collators, optical scanners.

Operations:

—experienced in processing information from tabulating cards into printed data; duplicating tapes and units from taped programs; can select and load machines with appropriate processing devices (card, disk, tape, drum); can initiate duplicating process from first steps of readying equipment, observe machine for malfunctioning, remove jammed cards or tapes, route processed material to subsequent station; perform rudimentary maintenance and repair tasks utilizing wrenches and screwdriver; provide and maintain records of jobs completed; maintain controls on each job

Training/Supervision:

—supervised training program for high-school students and continuing education programs for advanced operators

Employer: Digital Information Services, Inc., Manchester, NH, 1975 to present

Education: Associate Degree, Manchester Junior College, Manchester, NH, 1975

References available upon request.

Willing to relocate.

Computers
Computer Analyst
Second-job-seeker
Type of resume: **functional**

Dayna Bowie
4305 Portero Drive Apt. 25A
San Francisco, CA 94132
(415) 554-7924

Career Goal: Computer Program Analyst with a data processing company in the Bay Area

Work Experience:

Computer Programmer (1979-present)

  * Converted bookkeeping and cost analysis systems for hospitals into computer
    programs; wrote detailed instructions and logic flow charts that were in turn
    converted into COBOL or Fortran IV; recommended hardware; developed data
    control procedures; programs required continuous checking and revision to
    maintain most accurate information; debugging was an often-recurring duty;
    reported on all programs when completed.

Computer Operator (1976-1979)

  * After three-month training program consisting of classroom work and
    intensive on-job experience, began operating and monitoring Burroughs B263
    and B3500 and Univac 1050-II; experienced with various processing devices;
    monitored consoles for deviations from standard; maintained controls; solved
    operational problems and assisted in making corrections; checked out new
    programs.

Employer: Smithfield Electronics, San Francisco, CA

Education: B.S. in Accounting with a strong minor in computer technology,
              University of Southern California, Los Angeles, 1976

Personal: Single
              Health good

References available upon request.

Sam Richfield
4593 Euclid Ave.
South Bend, Indiana 46638
(219) 450-6733

Objective: System Analyst

Language: Fortran, COBOL, ANS COBOL

Hardware: IBM-360/20, 30
Honeywell-316, 516
Burroughs-2500, 3500

Applications: Analyzed business procedures to convert data into programs in the following areas—accounting, payroll scales, purchasing, production control, inventory, distribution, scheduling.

Accomplishments:

* improved existing data-handling systems
* increased effectiveness and work flow
* ascertained output requirements of organizational units
* devised efficient formats for management reports
* developed new systems to streamline work units
* explained clearly and in detail operations to be performed by computer personnel
* specified accurately the mathematical operations to be performed by equipment units
* studied, proposed, and evaluated new information systems to handle current and projected needs
* prepared technical reports advising the installation of future systems
* wrote instructional manuals for establishment and operation of complete systems
* developed data control procedures
* converted tape systems to disk-oriented ones

Work History:

1977-present	Systems Analyst, Elkhart Data Processing Consultants, South Bend, Indiana
1971-1977	Computer Programmer, Glen Valley Products, Indianapolis, Indiana
1967-1971	Computer Programmer, Greenfield Electronics, Indianapolis, Indiana

Education:
B.S. in Computer Sciences, Indiana University, Bloomington, Indiana, 1967

Construction
Carpentry Supervisor
Career-changer
Type of resume: **chronological**
Special circumstances: because of the death of his partner and the general economic malaise of the area, John was forced to dissolve his small company and seek employment with a larger company; see cover letter page 174.

John Wade
3496 Harbert Ave.
Grand Rapids, MI 49511
(616) 435-2299

Objective: Carpentry supervisor for large construction company

1976-1981	Wade and Sloan Subcontractors, President

—specialized in carpentry work and residential/commercial painting
—employed 15 workers
—completed projects for over 30 companies in Grand Rapids area
—acquired outstanding reputation for profitable estimates and projects completed within specified time frame

Projects included
—Hillside Estates Residential Homes
—Grant Plaza Doctors' Clinic
—Superior Cove Condominiums

1970-1976	John Wade Carpentry, President

—built and remodeled houses, garages, small commercial buildings
—employed 6 workers
—subcontracted by over 20 companies in Grand Rapids
—created good relations with personnel and project supervisors

Projects included
—Hartstown Senior Citizens' Center
—Flower Hills Apartments
—Westend Medical Center

1967-1970	Hendricks Construction Company, Carpentry Foreman

—hired as carpenter on leaving Army
—promoted to foreman in two years
—worked on residential buildings

Education: Grand Rapids Polytechnic College (1966-69)
Night courses in blueprint reading, welding, cutting, drafting, estimating, mortgages and taxes

Military Service: United States Army, 1964-66

Philip Wilkie
4593 Senate Street
Little Rock, AR 72214
(501) 354-6692

Goal: Construction Superintendent

Experience:

Superintendent of General Construction   1977-present

      J.P. Mallory and Sons, Little Rock, AR

    —responsibilities included: supervise entire construction projects; hire and fire workers;
direct and coordinate work of up to 95 workers through individual foremen; directly
supervise carpentry and masonry projects; subcontract work in electrical, plumbing,
etc.; approve all purchases; personally purchase all carpentry and masonry materials;
make reports; meet deadlines successfully

Carpentry Foreman   1973-76

      Frank Morris Contracting Company, Hot Springs, AR

    —supervised carpentry work on two major shopping centers; prepared progress reports;
met deadlines; maintained high morale among 15 carpenters

Carpenter   1963-73

      Fortex Contractors, Hot Springs, AR

    —hired as junior carpenter after four years on-the-job training and 128 classroom hours
at Apprentice Program, Local Carpenters Union; six years experience as carpenter on
jobs ranging in size from private homes to apartment complexes and shopping centers

Mechanical Artist   1961-63

      Welco Architects, Little Rock, AR

    —skills include blueprint reading, drafting, industrial design, tracing

Education:

    LaGrange High School, Pine Bluff, AR   1958
      —mechanical art major

Military:

    United States Navy   1959-61

Construction
Career-changer
Type of resume: **combination**
Special circumstances: Billie Lee is seeking an executive
position with a large construction company after a long career as
director/supervisor of construction projects

Billie Lee Marshall
159 Glen Oaks Drive
Rochester, NY 14612
(716) 756-0386

Career Goal: Assistant to the Vice-President of Marketing

Areas of Knowledge:

General contracting	Hiring and training
Subcontracting	Sales
Estimating	Customer relations
Financing	Field supervision
Building permits	Quality control analysis
Contracts	Purchasing
Labor relations	General business management

Education:

1957	State Technical College, Rochester, NY Major: Building Construction
1958-59	Apprenticeship, Carpenters Union, Rochester, NY
1975-78	Genesee Community College, Rochester, NY Advanced course for home builders: a six-semester program covering topics such as real estate, estimating, business law, contracts, etc.

Former Employers:

1978-present	Black and Sons, General Contractors, Inc. Rochester, NY	Project Director
1977-78	Comstock and Logan, General Contractors Rochester, NY	Field Supervisor
1969-77	Pete Salsbury, Carpentry Rochester, NY	Carpenter (2 years) Foreman (6 years)

Projects since 1977 include:

Bloomfield Junior High School, Bloomfield, NY	Project Director
Webster Community College, Rochester, NY	Project Director
Oneida Plaza Shopping Center, Rochester, NY	Field Supervisor
Niagara Church of God, Brockport, NY	Project Director

Credit Clerk
First-job-seeker/recent college graduate
Type of resume: **functional**

Frederick Cauldwell
2311 Stonewall Ave.
Memphis, TN 38104
(901) 354-7792

OBJECTIVE: Credit Clerk or Collections Assistant in credit department of a large department
store

EXPERIENCE:

Credit Clerk   Student Loan Department, Christian Brothers College, Business Office
(student-worker program)

* assisted Director of Student Loans in processing government loan applications

* helped students fill out loan application forms

* received and recorded loan payments from students

Treasurer of Student Government

* created operating budget for student government

* chaired Budget Approval Committee to determine legitimacy of student
organization budgets

* allocated funds targeted for specified groups/activities

* reviewed financial reports of student organizations

* kept accounts payable and receivable

* routinely calculated and posted student government financial accounts

* shared check-writing authority with student government vice-president

Teller   First Tennessee Bank, Memphis

* part-time teller at drive-up window

* handled deposits and withdrawals for checking and savings accounts

EDUCATION:

B.S. in Business Administration and Accounting
Christian Brothers College, Memphis, 1983

THOMAS DUNLAP   5649 Shrewsbury   Minneapolis, MN 55401   (612) 549-1176

Objective: Credit Manager

Skills and Achievements:

* establishes credit and collection systems
* supervises all credit requests
* interviews applicants for credit and collects necessary information for granting credit
* makes intensive studies of clients' financial statements and past credit records
* has full authority over delinquent accounts
* tactfully knows when to press for collections
* works with sales force to develop credit policy that will increase business
* supervises 20-person office
* has reduced delinquent accounts by 12 percent
* has reduced time for processing customer adjustments from three weeks to 10-12 days
* has reduced credit department staff by 5 people
* has improved reporting process by simplifying report form
* has successfully built up and maintained good customer relations
* has kept losses substantially below the projected sales percentages
* has reduced turnover in personnel, thereby creating a more stable and harmonious credit staff

Work Record:

1974-present	Solokow, Wilkins, and Larsen, Inc., St. Paul, MN	Credit Manager
1970-1974	St. Paul Mercantile Credit Corporation, St. Paul, MN	Assistant Credit and Collections Manager
1968-1970	Associated Foods, Inc., Minneapolis, MN	Credit Clerk

Education:

1968	B.A., University of Minnesota, cum laude
1972	Seminar in Financial Statement Analysis, Mendola College, St. Paul, MN
1980	Computer Programming Workshop, Mendola College, St. Paul, MN

References available upon request.

Nutritionist
First-job-seeker/housewife
Type of resume: **functional**

Rosemary Calle
14 Cactus Drive
Tucson, Arizona 85701
(416) 245-8384

Job Objective: Assistant Nutritionist for Tucson Public School District

Education:

B.S. in Nutrition, Arizona State College, 1976
Home Economics Major, Hidalgo High School, Tucson, 1960

Experience:

* Teacher in Home Economics I and II at Lakewood High; conducted one kitchen
  laboratory course each semester; supervised field trips to restaurants, hospitals,
  and hotels.

* Instructor of six-week course on Mexican cooking at Forty Carrots, Green Mesa Plaza.

* Research Assistant to Dr. Ruth Barberi on her book The Food You Eat; surveyed
  current popular literature; interviewed restaurant managers, physicians, nurses,
  mothers, chefs, children; collated material; prepared statistical charts used in text.

* Dining Hall Director at Camp Winslow, Eureka, New Mexico; prepared menus for
  three meals a day for 120 campers and staff of 50; ordered all food, equipment,
  and supplies; supervised 3 cooks and 2 busboys; made out work schedules.

* Contributor to Tucson Sun Times; occasional articles on nutrition; reviews of books
  on food and health.

* Cafeteria Cook at St. Ambrose Catholic School.

References:

Dr. Ruth Barberi, Arizona State College, Tucson, AZ
Wilfred Klemp, Principal, Lakewood High, Tucson, AZ
Jennie Dillon, Camp Director, Camp Winslow, Eureka, NM
Patricia Strafford, Manager, Forty Carrots Boutique, Green Mesa Plaza, Tucson, AZ

Dietitian
Career-changer
Type of resume: **functional**
Special circumstances: after a long career as a dietitian and
nutritionist, Louise is seeking an administrative position with the
American Heart Association.

LOUISE MCPHEE   421 Germantown Road   Cincinnati, OH 43215   (513) 564-1134

Objective: Administrative position with American Heart Association

NUTRITION COUNSELOR
   —counseled heart patients and their families regarding convalescent diets for home meals
   —wrote series of pamphlets on food and heart care for local chapter of heart association
   —wrote and prepared five video tapes on proper use and care of equipment in institutional
     kitchens
   —prescribed special dietary requirements for elderly in nursing homes
   —instructed day-care center personnel on principles of sound nutrition for children's
     meal program
   —in consultation with medical staff, selected proper meals to meet needs of patients
     while in hospital
   —recommended menus and eating schedules for professional athletes

RESEARCHER/TEACHER
   —conducted research experiments to improve nutritional quality of meals for the sick
     and elderly
   —organized programs to test the effects of various food groups on the elderly
   —conducted workshop on nutritional needs of the rural poor
   —lectured to various civic groups on the "natural" food craze
   —taught the following courses: Basic and Advanced Nutrition, Therapeutic Nutrition,
     Nutrition for Child Care Institutions, Nutrition for the Handicapped Child, Food
     Purchasing and Cost Control

FOOD SERVICE MANAGER
   —planned menus and supervised the preparation of meals for large and small institutions
   —hired and trained food service personnel
   —prepared and served special meals catering to the special needs of the elderly, handicapped,
     the ill, and children

Work Experience:

1974-present	Dietitian, Pleasant Hill Nursing Home, Cincinnati
1968-1974	Assistant Professor, Department of Nutrition, University of Ohio, Dayton
1963-1968	Therapeutic Dietitian, Suburban General Hospital, Pittsburgh, PA
1960-1963	Food Service Manager, Agaboo Foods, St. Mary-of-the-Woods College, Terre Haute, IN

Education:
   M.S. in Food and Nutrition, Ohio State University, 1968
   B.S. in Home Economics, Indiana State University, 1960

ADA Registry 1975
Ohio Dietetic Association
Cincinnati Heart Association

Research nutritionist
Second-job-seeker
Type of resume: **skill-based**

Evelyn Rogers
2830 Oakdale Road
Bethesda, Maryland 20857
(301) 345-6920

JOB TARGET: Research Nutritionist for Project 2000,
United States Department of Agriculture

Work Experience:

University of Maryland, School of Agriculture, 1981-83

Summary: Two-year research and development program in the field of ecology and food production, testing the effects of various fertilizers, soil nutrients, and climatic conditions on the nutritional value of standard food dishes; proposals for alternative food combinations and innovative menus; determination of acceptable food substitutes and their physical and psychological impact on human beings; project funded by the National Science Foundation.

Skills:

* determine the parameters of the problem to be studied

* devise suitable methodology and tools to carry out experiments

* establish control groups against which to evaluate data

* survey and utilize the existing literature

* apply current research discoveries

* supervise assistant researchers

* confer and share findings with other members of research team

* interpret results for a lay audience

Education:

M.A. in Nutrition, Johns Hopkins, Baltimore, 1979
B.S. in Life Sciences, University of Baltimore, 1976

See attached list of publications.

References available on request.

Draftsman
Job-changer
Type of resume: **combination chronological with heavy focus
on functional aspects**

Winslow Truman
3968 Frontview Blvd.
Toledo, Ohio 43649
(419) 898-3412

Objective: Supervisory position in drafting department of company specializing in camera or optical products

Experience:

Bell and Howell, Toledo, Ohio 1967-present	<u>Senior Draftsman</u> Sketched finished designs of basic parts of video components for marine cameras; served on research team for NASA contract studying video equipment to be used in Apollo projects; provided detailed sketches for remote-controlled cameras used outside spacecraft; worked on other projects involving high-speed precision photographic equipment <u>Supervising Draftsman</u> Headed drafting team designing micro-video components for surgical equipment; authorized to select and purchase parts and materials to fit specifications; handled all correspondence with suppliers
Arco Surgical Equipment Corp., Columbus, Ohio 1963-1967	Began as <u>junior drafter</u> responsible for sketches of precision surgical equipment; position provided excellent training in gross and detailed design work, including microscopic components; acquired invaluable knowledge of electrical and optical materials (base metals and synthetics); promoted after two years to <u>senior drafter</u> which included responsibilities for all charts representing statistical data

Education:

1963	Kettering Institute of Design, Dayton, Ohio Associates Degree in Drafting
1960	Dayton Vocational High School Four years of mechanical drawing and industrial design courses.

References available upon request.

Draftsman
First-job-seeker/recent college graduate
Type of resume: **functional**
Special circumstances: Randy is capitalizing on his military and
college internship experience to lend him a level II rather than a
level I position.

Randy Baker
5402 Holmes Street
Camden, NJ 08632
(609) 305-2957

Job Goal: Draftsman II level position with architectural firm in the Philadelphia area

Experience:

Assistant Tracer, Harting Associates, Philadelphia, 10/81-present

College internship program on state reconstruction projects (bridges, highways)
scheduled to end in May, 1982; was retained by Harting as salaried draftsman until
completion of Pennsauken Bridge project in October, 1982.

Junior Draftsman, United States Army, 8/77-8/80

After basic training, served as junior draftsman with Army Corps of Engineers on
harbor renovation projects in Mobile, Alabama.

Education:

1982   Associate Degree in Architectural Drafting
       Wodenbury College, Blackwood, NJ

1977   Mechanical Drawing Major
       Bailey Vocational High, Camden, NJ

Areas of Knowledge:

Architectural Drafting, Mechanical Drawing, Descriptive Geometry, Trigonometry,
Physics, Basic Electronics, Industrial Design

Personal:

Single
Health excellent
Interests: white-water rafting, fishing, hunting

References available on request.

Fashion
Career-changer
Type of resume: **skill-based**
Special circumstances: after twelve years experience of working
with furniture in terms of fashion and design, Randy is applying
for a buyer's position in a furniture department of a large store.

Randy Bruckner
4590 Hudson Ave. Apt. 23
Albany, NY 12231
(518) 929-3334

Job Target: Assistant Buyer for furniture department in a large department store

Skills: <u>Purchasing</u>

                —select merchandise for retail market

                —predict fashion trends

                —promote new fashions

                —examine merchandise and analyze competitive products

                —determine prices and markups

                —analyze furniture for defective design

                —spot material and structural imperfections

                <u>Administrative</u>

                —handle purchase orders

                —maintain inventory control

                —function as liaison between sources and department supervisors

                —prepare and operate within a set budget

Work History:

1978-present   Wolf Interior Design, Albany, NY
                —designer and decorator, business manager
1974-1978   Handley's Furniture Company, Albany, NY
                —fabric designer
1968-1974   Yesterday's Antiques, Saratoga Springs, NY
                —shop assistant, furniture restorer

Education:
1968   Trenton High School, Utica, NY

References available upon request.

Fashion design
Job-changer
Type of resume: **chronological**
Special circumstances: because she is looking for work in the
Detroit area, Joycelin uses the chronological resume to highlight
two well-known department stores for which she has worked.

Joycelin Andrews
9238 Dearborn St. Apt. 24
Sterling Heights, MI 48215
(313) 278-1145

Objective: Fashion Coordinator

Employment:

1978-present   Hudson's Department Store, Detroit

Fashion Coordinator
—responsible for 10 to 12 major fashion shows annually; determined
fashion themes, hired models; selected clothes, contracted caterers,
musicians, and other fashion show personnel; promoted new fashions;
studied fashion journals; attended garment conventions; visited
manufacturers; consulted with buyers in major departments; held
department head meetings to determine seasonal themes.

1975-1978   Benchley's Department Store, Detroit

Display Supervisor (1976-1978)
—supervised staff of six display personnel responsible for approximately
30 separate in-store displays; coordinated seasonal window displays;
designed wall, counter, and island displays; coordinated activities with
public relations and advertising departments.

Display Assistant (1975-1976)
—dressed windows, mannequins, prepared decorations and accessories,
assisted with clothing preparations.

Education:

    1975   B.A. in Design, Royal Oak Academy of Arts, Pontiac, MI
    1979   Advanced Certificate in Design, Detroit Institute of Design, Detroit

References available upon request.

Portfolio available.

Fashion designer
First-job-seeker/recent college graduate
Type of resume: **combination**

Marie Bently
281 Greenwich St. Apt. 5-D
New York, NY 10013
(212) 352-6693

Position: Assistant Fashion Designer in women's clothing

Education:

M.A. in Fashion Design
Wentworth School of Design, Boston, 1983

B.A. in Art
Columbia University, New York, 1979

Skills:

Fashion design for men, women, and children

Pattern design for fabric

Evaluation and selection of fabrics appropriate for style and article of clothing

Sewing

Jewelry crafting

Work Experience:

Abraham and Straus, Brooklyn, NY

Assistant Fashion Coordinator for four seasonal fashion shows (1979)

Display Assistant: prepared clothing for display on mannequins; collected and mounted window accessories; occasionally advised supervisor on window dressings (part-time, 1977-78)

Vogue magazine, New York City
Summer Internship: researcher and design assistant on promotional brochure (1979)

Portfolio and references available on request.

Financial Consultant
Career-changer
Type of resume: **skill-based**
Special circumstances: after a long career in research and
consulting firms, Gerald is seeking a job in industry.

Gerald Stefano
3589 Longhorn Avenue
Houston, Texas 77013
(713) 997-1135

Position: Director of Financial Management Services

Financial Planning:

—long- and short-range financial forecasting; capital investment opportunities;
feasibility studies; acquisition; financial projections; budgets; tax reductions

Market Research:

—consumer surveys; policy formulation; sales potentials; advertising concepts and
implementation strategies; transportation and distribution costs

Statistical Analysis:

—innovative statistical methodologies and analysis; trend analysis; geographic-
demographic distributions; media evaluation; survey designs

Product Development:

—product costs forecasting; pricing policies; intradivisional resource allocation;
costing techniques; research and development budgeting; feasibility studies;
packaging

Employment Record

1970-present   Armo Data Research, Houston, TX
                   Senior Financial Analyst

1964-1970   Texas Research, Inc., Houston, TX
                   Financial Analyst/Financial Planner

Education

M.A. in Financial Planning, Rice University, Houston, 1964

B.A. in Accounting, Monroe College, Monroe, Louisiana, 1961

References available on request.

Berkley Winston
5693 London Street
Toledo, Ohio 43641
(419) 898-2256

Position: Director of Profit Planning

Work History:

1971-present   Pontiac Looms, Inc., Toledo, Ohio

Corporate Budget Manager (1975-present)
—created corporate and departmental operating budgets; established five-year profit
plan, consolidated and coordinated all periodic financial reports; calculated cash
requirements and evaluated capital expenditures; analyzed and reported on factory
overheads; invested in short-term commercial paper; handled company insurance
programs (pension plans, stock options and profit-sharing program)

Senior Budget Analyst (1971-1975)
—forecasted annual profit plan; established responsibility accounting for industry cost
centers; consolidated monthly forecasts; prepared monthly variance reports; reconciled
persistent problem areas; converted to data processing system; reduced monthly
closing times by four days

1967-1971   Wendel Electronics, Dayton, Ohio

Market Research Analyst
—prepared commodity charts and market strategies; identified applications for transistor
technologies in television, radio, and telecommunications; forecasted annual industry
demand for products; evaluated potential acquisitions

Education:

M.A. in Marketing, Indiana State University, Bloomington, Indiana, 1967

B.S. in Accounting, University of Chicago, 1963

Executive Seminar in Financial Planning, University of Ohio at Toledo, 1974

References available upon request.

Health Care
Dental Hygienist
Second-job-seeker
Type of resume: **skill-based**

Marjorie Swackman   8347 Mountainview   Butte, Mt 59781   (406) 242-8837

Objective: position as dental hygienist with opportunity to develop instructional
materials to increase public awareness regarding proper dental care

Capabilities:

EXAMINATION AND TREATMENT
—sterilize and disinfect instruments and equipment
—prepare tray setup
—chart mouths
—perform oral prophylaxis
—administer fluoride treatments
—prepare materials for making impressions
—place and remove dressings
—take and develop X rays
—perform routine laboratory procedures

PATIENT EDUCATION
—demonstrate proper brushing, flossing, mouthwashing procedures
—explain postoperative instructions as determined by physician
—instruct parents on relationship between foods and growing teeth and the
special needs of children, especially instilling good dental hygiene habits at an
early age
—develop and illustrate programs to teach children the facts about teeth and
tooth decay
—motivate patients to be concerned about preventive tooth care

RECORD KEEPING
—take patient histories
—keep records accurate and up-to-date
—bill patients
—make appointments

Former Employer:

George Thompson, DDS, Butte, Montana   1978-present

Education:

Associates Degree in Dental Hygiene   1977
Helena Junior College, Helena, Montana

References available from employer and former patients on request.

First-job-seeker/recent college graduate
Type of resume: **skill-based**

Carol Dolan
5490 Pine Street Apt. 4
Eugene, Oregon 97412
(503) 658-1139

Job Objective: Medical Assistant for doctor in private practice or small clinic

Education:

Medical Assistant Program 1982
Cascade Community College
Eugene, Oregon

Internship

—300 hours in emergency room, surgical floor, out-patient clinic, and medical records at Marcus Whitman General Hospital, Eugene, OR

Courses

—Administrative Skills

Scheduling patients, interviewing, taking patient histories, maintaining medical records, typing and medical transcriptions, routine office management, handling phone calls and correspondence.

—Clinical Skills

Preparing patients for examination, obtaining vital signs, sterilizing instruments, preparing patients for X rays, carrying out routine lab procedures, CPR, EKG, IV's, assisting with medical examinations and minor surgery, instructing patients in post-op care.

Licensed by National Certification Board 1983

Member: American Association of Medical Assistants

Personal: Born March 17, 1961
Single
Health good

Willing to relocate on West Coast.

References available on request.

Medical Records Administrator
Job-changer
Type of resume: **skill-based**
Special circumstances: after founding and administering a
medical records department, Madelyn must leave position to
accompany her husband to another part of country; job objective
omitted because she hopes that with her extensive experience, a
health care institute will create some position for her. See cover
letter p. 167.

Madelyn Owen   4593 Fremont Ave.   Kansas City, MO 64115   (816) 540-3394

Summary: Ten years as Director of Medical Records Department at the Colorado
                      Heart Institute; hired to create medical records system when the Heart
                      Institute was founded; since then it has served as a leading model for
                      other health data systems.

Areas of Experience:

Planning: created and developed entire medical records system for C.H.I. when it was
                      founded in 1972; implemented policies and procedures in conformance
                      with federal, state, and local statutes; received high rating from
                      accrediting agencies and met standards of state regulatory board on each
                      succeeding review.

Supervision: directly responsible for staff of five; for documenting, storing, and
                      retrieving all information on patients and the Heart Institute; for
                      handling and processing legal documents and insurance forms; for filing
                      copies of pertinent correspondence.

Analysis: assisted medical staff and heads of nonmedical departments in evaluating
                      quality of patient care and progress of individual therapy programs;
                      developed criteria and methodology for patient evaluation in consultation
                      with staff.

Education: developed and administered in-house educational service; in conjunction
                      with medical library, made available educational materials, latest
                      research, appropriate studies, journal articles; supervised and conducted
                      training programs for new health care personnel.

Consulting: acted as liaison with other health care organizations (hospitals, clinics,
                      government agencies) in collecting medical data; provided consultant
                      services to other health institutes regarding medical record systems; C.H.I.
                      system frequently studied by outsiders and considered to be one of the
                      most efficiently organized and administered in the nation.

Education: M.A. in Biology, University of Ohio, Columbus, 1966

Employers: Colorado Heart Institute, Denver, CO, 1972-1982
                      Deaconness Hospital, St. Louis, MO, 1969-1972

Personal: Birthdate May 8, 1944
                      Married, one child
                      Health good

References available upon request.

Health Care
Nurse
Job-changer/re-entering
Type of resume: **functional**
Special circumstances: older woman re-entering nursing profession;
see cover letter p. 171.

Rosemary Furlong
549 Diana Street
Nashville, TN 37218
(615) 232-5594

Objective: to contribute experience and expertise of a long, distinguished career in nursing
by re-entering profession as a mature, experienced nurse or nursing supervisor

Experience:

Director of Nursing Services   University of Tennessee Medical School Hospitals

—built a nursing staff that was greatly admired throughout hospital; established an effective
nurses' aid program; maintained excellent working relationship with doctors and staff;
emergency room nursing staff won reputation as providing best emergency service in city.
1962-1965

Operating Room Supervisor

—after one year assisting surgeons in operating room, appointed supervisor of student
nurses for surgery; maintained OR supplies; established nurses' schedules; assigned daily
cases to nursing staff.
1955-1962

United States Army Nurse   Korea

—general nursing care for U.S. military personnel and their families; took histories, kept
charts, prepared patients for tests, surgery, administered medication.
1952-1954

Staff Nurse   St. Cecilia's Hospital, Dayton, OH

—prepared patients for operations; administered medications; monitored progress; assisted
in physical and medical therapy.
1950-1952

Education:

Nursing Diploma, University of Ohio, School of Nursing, 1950

References available upon request.

Health Care
Nurse
Second-job-seeker
Type of resume: **skill-based**

Judy Reagan
3490 Whiteside Drive Apt. 5-J
Flint, Michigan 48512
(313) 692-4179

Job Objective: Nursing position in Intensive Care Unit

Experience:

INTENSIVE CARE TREATMENT

* can recognize and treat special needs of post-op patients; assist doctors in post-op treatment; provide physical and medical therapy for recovery

CARDIAC PATIENT CARE

* experienced in cardiac technology and needs of heart patients; can provide therapy for stroke and heart attack victims

GENERAL NURSING FUNCTIONS

* take histories; prepare patients for testing, surgery, treatment; administer medication; tend to patients' needs

Present Position:

Pontiac County Hospital   Flint, Michigan

Cardiac Care Center

Intensive Care Unit

Education:

1978 R.N. Detroit School of Nursing, Detroit, MI

1975 B.A. in Liberal Arts   Xavier College, Detroit, MI

Personal:

Birthdate—December 12, 1956

Single

Willing to relocate

References available upon request.

Dorothy Heitert   6594 Winter Lane   Milwaukee, WI 53248   (414) 454-3306

Career Goal: Teaching position at St. Luke's School of Nursing

1976-present	Consultant/Lecturer	Milwaukee Research Hospital

—appointed head of new program in medical ethics; provided consulting services to other hospitals, medical schools, and health care centers; conducted workshops and seminars on treatment of the terminally ill; expanded internship for training health care professionals in counseling and caring for the dying patient; part-time lecturer at University of Milwaukee Medical School.

1972-1976   Cancer Ward Supervisor

—supervised staff of 25 nurses; made up daily and weekly work schedules; instituted training program for providing health care to the terminally ill.

1970-1972   Assistant Head Nurse   Omaha State Psychiatric Institute

—in charge of in-service education and nursing internship program; did individual therapy and group therapy.

1967-1970   Assistant Supervisor

—in charge of 15 personnel in cancer ward; took histories, kept charts; prepared patients for surgery; administered medication.

1961-1962   Staff Nurse   St. Elizabeth's Hospital, Omaha

—after one year of general nursing, returned to school for Master's degree.

Education: 1966 M.S.N., University of Wisconsin at Milwaukee
             1961 B.S. in Nursing, Creighton University, Omaha

Publications: "Counseling the Dying Patient," Midwest Medical Journal, Spring, 1980.

"Health Care for the Terminally Ill: Are We Meeting Their Needs?" Midwest Medical Journal, Fall, 1979.

"The Place to Die: Home or Hospital?" Xaverian Journal of Ethics, Winter, 1977.

Associations: American Nursing Association
                Wisconsin State Nursing Association
                American Organization of Psychiatric Nurses

References available upon request.

Roger Landon
356 West 4th Street Apt. 5-D
New York, NY 10011
(212) 545-3306

Job Objective: Paramedic with New York City Emergency Medical Service

Skills:

Control of Bleeding
Shock Treatment
Maintenance of Airway
Cardiopulmonary Resuscitation
Defibrillation
Intubation
Emergency Baby Delivery
IV and Drug Administration
Scene Evaluation
Ambulance Driver

Temperament:

Emotional Stability
Physical Stamina
Clear Thinking
Sincere Concern for People
Realistic Appreciation of Physical Danger

Experience:

St. Francis Hospital Buffalo, NY	1976-1983
—Paramedic	
Auburn General Hospital Auburn, NY	1974-1975
—Internship Program	
United States Army Vietnam, Purple Heart	1968-1972
—Paramedic	

Education:

Syracuse Junior College Syracuse, NY	1972-1975
—Paramedic Certificate	

References available on request.

Health Care
Physical Therapist
Second-job-seeker
Type of resume: **skill-based**
Special circumstances: Gladys is deaf. See cover letter p. 175.

Gladys Greene
5039 Peachtree Street
Macon, Georgia 31244
(912) 939-8847

Position: Rehabilitation Therapist

Skills:

* diagnose sprains, strains, ruptures

* test range of motion, strength, endurance, and functional analysis

* measure parts of body for height, weight, fat ratios

* plan appropriate treatment for injuries

* administer light, water, heat, and electrotherapy

* use ultrasound and diathermy equipment

* administer and regulate traction equipment

* instruct loss-of-limb patients in use, care, and benefits of prosthetic devices

* prepare and adjust home care programs to fit in with daily activities of patients and their families

* keep accurate records of treatment, sessions, and progress

Work Record:

1979 to present	Macon General Hospital, Macon, Georgia
1978	University of Savannah Medical Center, Savannah, Georgia
	Internship Program

Education:

| 1978 | B.S. in Physical Therapy |
| | University of Savannah, Savannah, Georgia |

Willing to relocate.

References available on request.

James Warner
5938 Wingate Parkway
Kansas City, MO 64113
(816) 549-5592

Goal: Position as Director of Physical Therapy

Physical Therapist   Kansas City Rehabilitation Center   1975-present
                          Kansas City, Missouri

   —perform and interpret diagnostic tests on heart patients; plan and administer
    therapy programs, including treadmill, calisthenics, jogging, etc.; supervise staff of
    five; responsible for periodic checking of therapy patients to adjust programs
    according to progress made; conduct public workshops on exercise and heart care at
    Institute; lecture on exercise to local civic, church groups, and high schools

Assistant Physical   Lutheran Hospital   1973-1975
  Therapist   Kansas City, Missouri

   —worked in children's ward administering post-op therapy, including swimming and
    group games

Part-time Physical   Southgate Care Center   1972-1973
  Therapist   Shawnee Mission, Kansas

   —internship program involving work with geriatric residents, many recovering from
    strokes and heart attacks

Education:

    Physical Therapist Certificate, Dekalb University, Kansas City   1973

    B.A. in Physical Education, University of Missouri, Columbia, MO   1970

Personal:

    Born 1950

    Single

    Interests: sports of all kinds, innovative methods in education, movies, travel

References available on request.

Health Care
Respiratory Therapist/ECG Technician
Second-job-seeker
Type of resume: **skill-based**

Barbara Terasso
5493 East Main Street
Davenport, Iowa 52816
(319) 565-3395

Position: Respiratory Therapist or Electrocardiograph Technician, wish to work 25-30 hours
per week.

Skills and Experience

General respiratory therapy
Artificial ventilation therapy
Chest physiotherapy
Airway maintenance
Cardiopulmonary resuscitation
Electrocardiograph procedures
Evaluation of electrocardiograms
Ventilator installation
Pulmonary function examinations
Blood tests
Stress tests
"Code Blue" procedures
Patient education

Former Employer

Quad Cities General Hospital   1979-present
Davenport, Iowa

Education

Amana Junior College   1979
Associate Degree in Respiratory Therapy
Internship at McBride Hospital, Cedar Rapids, Iowa

Roosevelt High School   1977
Cedar Rapids, Iowa

Personal

Born February 12, 1959
Married, two children

References available on request.

Bart Weathers
596 Pawnee Blvd. Apt. 4
Oklahoma City, OK 73192
(405) 838-5592

Objective: Claims Adjuster for an insurance company

Work Record:

1979-present   Claims Adjuster   Shawnee Fire Insurance Co.
                                                     Oklahoma City, OK

                  —full responsibility for obtaining on-the-scene data from investigators and
                    statements from witnesses, making complete assessment of property
                    damage, determining liability, and negotiating final settlements

1976-1979   Office Claims Representative

                  —responsibilities included receiving and processing claim forms from
                    policy holders; confirming coverage, issuing settlement drafts

1973-1976   Claims Investigator   Arco Insurance Co.
                     (auto insurance)   Oklahoma City, OK

                  —learned on-the-spot procedures for inspecting damaged property,
                    obtaining necessary photos, preparing damage estimates, and
                    negotiating agreed prices with repair shops

Education:

  1973   B.A. in Liberal Arts with a minor in Business Administration

                  University of Oklahoma, Stillwater

Member: National Association of Public Adjusters, Oklahoma City

Personal:

                  Birthdate: February 11, 1953
                  Single
                  Interests: horseback riding, wood carving

References available upon request.

Claims Manager
Job-changer
Type of resume: **skill-based with achievements**
Special circumstances: Edward is seeking relocation in
hometown with smaller company after suffering a heart attack.

Edward Taylor
4502 Avenue U Apt. 16-B
Brooklyn, NY 10012
(212) 898-3385

Career Target: Claims Administrator with a small insurance company in the Milwaukee area

Capabilities:

* handle and supervise complicated claims negotiations in life, pensions, fire, and theft

* hire and train adjusters

* develop new sales methods that lead to substantial increase

* supervise sales persons

* organize office activities for maximum work flow

Achievements:

* added 25 new major accounts in nine-month period

* named Agent of the Month seven times

* reduced customer complaints by 51 percent in four-year period

* revised underwriting manual and devised simpler claims forms

* created underwriting training program

* trained many claims adjusters over the years who are now serving as claims managers

Employment History:

1974-present   Mutual of Omaha, Brooklyn, NY

1965-1974   Mutual of Omaha, Milwaukee, WI

1958-1965   Nationwide Insurance Company, Milwaukee, WI

Education:

    1958   M.A. in Constitutional Law, University of Wisconsin, Madison

    1955   B.A. in History, Marquette University, Milwaukee, WI

References available upon request.

Insurance Adjuster
Career-changer
Type of resume: **chronological**
Special circumstances: Working for a small insurance company
where she knows there will be no openings for an underwriter,
Alice is seeking that position elsewhere.

Alice Peterson
5467 27th St. N.E.
Washington, D.C. 20013
(202) 884-5692

Job Objective: Position as underwriter with possible advancement to managerial duties

Work Experience:

Morris Underwriters, Inc., Washington, D.C.   (1978-present)

—began as assistant claims representative specializing in auto insurance and was
promoted in six months to senior claims representative; also experienced in
commercial properties; promoted to office supervisor, managing a staff of six
personnel

E. Burdick Associates, Washington, D.C.   (1976-1978)

—began the training program as junior insurance investigator and advanced to
assistant claims representative

Education:
1975   B.S. in Marketing
Silver Springs College, MD

1971   Hagerstown High School
Hagerstown, MD

Personal:
Date of Birth: October 21, 1955
Divorced
Willing to relocate

References available on request.

Laboratory Technician
First-job-seeker/recent college graduate
Type of resume: **functional**

Dale Perkins
8203 Lauderdale Ave.
Collierville, TN 38113
(901) 359-2299

Career Objective: Biochemical Technician

Experience

Research Laboratory Assistant   1981-1983

—on-going study of mosquito control in the Nonconnah Creek Basin, funded in part by
NSF and Shelby County Government; tested effects of new insecticides on mosquito
population and wildlife; developed new insecticides under direction of Professor Oswald
Schumacher.

Laboratory Assistant   1980-1981

—under the direction of Dr. Mustafa Rashid, Professor of Marine Biology; collected water
samples from McKellar Lake; performed lab experiments to determine changes in
oxygen level over a two-year period; traced marine life; ran chlorophyl tests on plant life.

Publications

"Born Again: Bringing Lake McKellar Back to Life,"
Tennessee Wildlife Journal, Winter, 1981.

"Hydrology and the Artesian Wells of Shelby County,"
Life Sciences, Spring, 1982.

Education

1983   Master's degree in Ecological Studies
Memphis State University, Memphis, TN

Thesis: "Ecological Rejuvenation of a Man-made Lake"

1980   Bachelor's degree in Biology
Memphis State University

Course Concentration:

Biology	Qualitative Organic Analysis
Organic Chemistry	Food Production
Principles of Ecology	Marine Biology
Bacteriology	Entomology

References available upon request.

Laboratory Technician
Second-job-seeker
Type of resume: **skill-based**

Regina Watkins
8932 Hudson Ave.
White Plains, NY 10613
(914) 989-3375

Objective: Lab Technician with possibility of advancement to supervisory position

Skills/Responsibilities

* set up and operate laboratory equipment

* run complex chemical and physical tests

* prepare test solutions and specimens

* monitor on-going tests, record data

* produce experimental samples of new foodstuffs

* establish and meet quality standards

* train apprentice lab technicians and supervise them in specific research assignments

* communicate results of tests for both professional and lay audiences

Research Areas

Low-calorie food and drink (taste control, chemical balances)
High-fiber cereals
Progressive cat and dog foods

Employer

General Foods, Inc., White Plains, NY, 1978-present

—began as assistant laboratory technician and was promoted after two years to full lab technician

Education

B.S. in Chemistry, cum laude, 1978
University of North Dakota
Fargo, ND

Willing to relocate.

References available on request.

Laboratory Technician/Medical Researcher
Job-changer
Type of resume: **chronological**
Special circumstances: Chronological resume used to highlight
prestigious employers and well-known supervisors.

Brian Sheahan
470 West End Parkway
Rye, New York 10513
(914) 402-4493

Career Goal: Senior Laboratory Technician in Medical Research

Work Experience:

1976-present   Sloane-Kettering, Rye, New York

—senior laboratory technician for a team headed by Dr. Sedgwick Price;
spent several months (1977) as consultant at St. Jude's Children's
Research Hospital, Memphis; delivered two papers to Senate Committee
on cancer research (1978, 1981).

1972-1976   Clinical Research Associates, New York, New York

—laboratory technician, worked under supervision of Dr. Kwang Fon,
specialist in dermatology; major research on treatment of rashes
caused by industrial pollutants.

1967-1972   Lederle Laboratories, Purchase, New York

—assistant laboratory technician, worked under Dr. Constance Turbo,
research involved the effects of various drugs on neurological
disorders.

Education

Ph.D. in Chemistry, Princeton University, 1967

B.A. in Life Sciences, Fordham University, 1962

Member: American Association of Medical Technologists
New York Institute for Cancer Research
International Society for the Study of Infectious Diseases

References available upon request.

See attached listing of publications.

Attorney
Second-job-seeker
Type of resume: **functional**
Special circumstances: an older woman, Christine returned to
law school after her children were grown; previous nonlegal
work experiences unnecessary for this resume

Christine Wendell
5592 Delaware Ave, Apt. 4-B
Washington, D.C. 20031
(202) 545-3305

Experience

Special Assistant to the General Counsel for Secretary Patricia Harris

Office of the Secretary, United States Department of Health and Human Services,
Washington, D.C.

—advised the Executive Secretary and other senior officials on legislation pertaining
to civil rights and health care; reviewed and reported to the General Counsel on
major developments in civil rights and health-welfare litigation within the
Department; drafted policy determination and position papers on Title VI of 1964
Civil Rights Act.

(September 1978-May 1981)

Counselor

Women's Center, Washington, D.C.

—volunteer four days a week, offering legal counsel to women who have suffered job
discrimination and who have been unfairly treated by lawyers or judges in divorce
cases.

(June 1981-present)

Education

LL.B. Howard University School of Law, 1978
Washington, D.C.

B.A. in Sociology, Wichita State University, 1961
Wichita, Kansas

Personal

Born: November 11, 1940
Married
Health excellent

References available on request.

Attorney
First-job-seeker/recent college graduate
Type of resume: **combination**

Bayard Coltrain
9384 St. Charles Street
New Orleans, LA 70139
(504) 993-5833

Objective: Attorney with law firm

EDUCATION

Juris Doctor, 1983
Loyola University, New Orleans, LA
Harriet Steele Lanford Scholarship

Bachelor of Arts, 1979
University of Mississippi, Oxford, MS
Major: History, cum laude
Class standing: 18 out of 340

COURSE CONCENTRATION IN JURIS DOCTOR DEGREE

Trial Practice	Corporate Law
Appeals	Criminal Law Procedures
Contracts	Trial Preparation
Wills and Trusts	Legal Research
Family Law	Juvenile Law
Taxes	Insurance Law

STUDENT ACTIVITIES

Junior Bar Association
Dean's List (U. of Miss and Loyola)
Debating Club, First Place Prize, 1979
Student-Faculty Discipline Committee
Student Court, Counsel
Swimming Team

PAPERS PUBLISHED

"Desegregation in Jefferon Parish: A Backward Glance,"
Louisiana Law Review, Spring, 1981

"A Children's Bill of Rights: What It Really Implies,"
Gulf Coast Scholastic, November, 1982

REFERENCES available upon request.

Legal Assistant/Law Clerk
Second-job-seeker
Type of resume: **combination emphasizing present employer**

Oliver Randall
659 Filmore Street
Grand Rapids, MI 49523
(616) 676-3392
(Evenings)

Position Desired: Legal Assistant for counsel with a federal government agency
involved in affirmative action suits

Present Employer

Lucas, Cable, and Finley
Grand Rapids, Michigan

(1981-present)

Law Clerk—

Major responsibility: writing and editing Amicus Curae brief
for J. Winston Lucas, who wrote Redford vs. University of Michigan,
reverse discrimination suit before Michigan Supreme Court

Capabilities:

Legal Research
Statistical Analysis
Client Interviews
Title Searches
Case Preparation
Investigations

Education

Legal Assistant Diploma
Flint Junior College, Detroit, MI
1981

B.A. in Political Science
University of Michigan, Lansing
1978

Personal

Born: January 15, 1958, Kalamazoo, Michigan
Marital Status: Married
Health: Good
Interests: History, folk music, Americana

Sarah Hunter
2948 San Bernardino Rd.
San Bernardino, CA 92417
(714) 565-3395

Career Goal: Position as Legal Assistant with a Los Angeles law firm

PROFESSIONAL EXPERIENCE

Legal Assistant and Statistical Analyst—Office of General Counsel, Office for Civil Rights, United States Department of Health, Education, and Welfare, Los Angeles

December 1979—present

Reviewed and reported to the Director of the Office for Civil Rights the compliance of state institutions of higher education with Title VI of 1964 Civil Rights Act; prepared pleadings and statistical analysis for school desegregation and hospital closure cases.

Investigator—Public Defender's Office, Los Angeles

May 1978—November 1979

Interviewed defendants and witnesses; collected pretrial testimony, photos, statements, and other data; evaluated and coordinated evidence; counseled public inquirers regarding legal rights, court proceedings, procedures for requesting and obtaining public defender.

EDUCATIONAL BACKGROUND

Associate Degree in Legal Assistant Program,
  Santa Monica Community College, Santa Monica CA
  1978

Claremont College, Los Angeles CA
  90 hours in History and Political Science
  1974-1976

REFERENCES AND WRITING SAMPLES

Furnished on request.

Librarian
First-job-seeker/recent college graduate
Type of resume: **skill-based.** See cover letter p. 169.

Joyce Langdon
4928 Chartres Street
New Orleans, Louisiana 70114
(504) 650-3589 (evenings)

Job Objective: Assistant Librarian in any department

Skills:

Research

Maintain and update files

Order and maintain audiovisual materials

Acquisition new books

Develop reading programs for special groups (children, senior citizens, civic
groups)

Teach use of card catalogs, research sections, reference books, and magazine
indexes

Experience:

Researcher (part-time) in reference section of University Library while
undergraduate

Internship in Children's Department, New Orleans Public Library, Metarie
Branch, while studying for Master's degree

Education:

M.S. in Library Science
Tulane University, New Orleans, 1983

B.S. in English,
Indiana University, Bloomington, 1979

References available on request.

Librarian
Career-changer
Type of resume: **chronological**
Special circumstances: after six years as corporate librarian John is
returning to the public library system; he uses chronological resume
to emphasize employment with a locally well-known company and
to point out that he has formerly worked for the public library
system.

JOHN CANASTA   1934 Smithe Lane   Denver, CO 80235   (303) 991-6306

Objective

Assistant Head Librarian, Department of Art and Architecture

Summary

Ten years experience as reference librarian in Art and Architecture and as corporate librarian
for a major Denver architectural firm

Experience

Holt Architectural Associates, Denver   1976-present

    Corporate Librarian

    —ordered books, pamphlets, magazines; cataloged books; maintained files; scanned
    periodicals and referred specific articles to appropriate divisions and departments;
    clipped and filed articles of permanent interest; researched and provided source
    material as requested by various departments; published quarterly newsletter listing
    new publications, studies, and recent acquisitions.

Denver Public Library, Sugarloaf Branch   1972-1976

    Reference Librarian

    —in charge of reference work in art and architecture department; serviced government
    documents; maintained files, films, and audiovisual materials; trained groups in use of
    reference sources.

Education

    B.S. in Library Science
    University of Colorado, Boulder, 1972

Member: American Library Association
          Colorado Association of Librarians

Personal

    Born 1946, Colorado Springs, CO
    Health excellent
    Single
    Hobbies: hiking, skiing, racketball

Mailroom clerk
Second-job-seeker
Type of resume: **functional**

James Weiss
4828 Eden Park Row
Cincinnati, Ohio 45217
(513) 939-2285

Objective: Mailroom Supervisor

Experience

Mailroom Clerk   University of Cincinnati   1976-present

    Responsibilities:

        * open, sort, and route mail

        * deliver mail to designated buildings and departments on campus

        * prepare letters and packages for mailing off campus

        * work closely with mail supervisor in opening and reading unspecified mail to
          determine individual or department for whom it is intended

        * compute postage costs for outgoing mail as determined by weight and
          classification

        * assist in preparing invoices reflecting each department's or area's monthly
          postal expenses

Mail Carrier   United States Postal Service   1975-1976
                        Dayton, Ohio

        * substituted on routes for regular carriers who were vacationing or absent due
          to illness

Education

    Mason Senior High, Mason, Ohio
    Graduated: 1974

Personal

    Born 1957

    Single

    Health excellent

References upon request.

Willing to relocate.

Frank Johnson
656 Wellington Place
Bismarck, North Dakota 58513
(701) 898-1155

POSITION: Mailroom Supervisor for private corporation

WORK HISTORY:

United States Postal Service
East Bismarck Station
Bismarck, North Dakota

Assistant Supervisor	1978-present
Window Clerk	1974-1978
Carrier	1967-1974

Skills:

—establish rules and regulations for postal clerks and mail carriers in accordance
with federal guidelines

—supervise receiving, opening, sorting of mail in main branch of city postal system

—supervise department heads

—hire and train new clerks

—responsible for 24-hour receiving and shipping services

—responsible for public notices, posters, informational displays, service brochures to
inform public of station's services

—maintain accurate budget records for salaries, overhead, and unforeseen expenses

EDUCATION:

Fort Lincoln High School, Bismarck, North Dakota, 1960

MILITARY:

United States Army, Second Lieutenant, 1960-1966

REFERENCES available on request.

Manufacturing/Plant Foreman
Second-job-seeker
Type of resume: **functional**

Peter Greenfield
5493 Mossy Rock Cove
Dayton, Ohio 45416
(513) 899-2248

Experienced Plant Foreman:

—supervised 12 operators, 4 metal sheet workers, 3 setup men

—coordinated work force of 40 at maximum over two shifts

—interviewed, hired, and trained all replacements

—improved organization and safety of shop through needed corrections

—directed work on heavy and light presses

—worked with brass, copper, bronze, steel, and other metals

—reduced downtime

—reduced rejection record by improving quality of finished products

—minimized customer complaints

—maintained high morale among workers

—reduced complaints brought to Employee Grievance Committee

Employer:

Halford Manufacturing, Inc., Dayton, Ohio

—manufacturers of industrial equipment; $85 million sales annually; employs over 1,000 workers

Foreman of Fabricating and Welding	1978-present
Machinist	1976-78

Education:

Bailey Vocational High School Fort Wayne, Indiana	1972

Military:

U.S. Army	1972-75

—worked with U.S. Army Corps of Engineers as welder, Fort Braske, Iowa

References available on request.

Ray Vosker
9485 Pasadina Drive
Modesto, CA 95319
(209) 656-3958

Position: Grounds and buildings supervisor for Carson University, Yosemite Campus

Capabilities and Experience

* industrial maintenance
* purchasing supplies and equipment
* cost control
* budget preparation
* inventory control
* loss and scrap control
* manpower allocation
* scheduling work crews
* staff supervision
* reducing work crew while maintaining quality results
* hiring and training
* labor relations
* union negotiations

Work History

Lemmel Industries, Modesto, CA

—manufacturers of household appliances; $28 million sales volume;
 700 employees

—Plant Manager	1975-present
—Manager of Quality Control	1970-1975

The Shea Corporation, Sonora, CA

—manufacturer of waste disposal equipment; annual sales $60 million;
 1,000 employees

—Plant Supervisor	1965-1970
—Foreman	1963-1965
—Machinist	1959-1963

Education

Eureka Trade School, Oakland, CA	1959
Berk High School, Sonora, CA	1958

References available.

Manufacturing/Purchasing Agent
Second-job-seeker
Type of resume: **skill-based**

Philip Giljohn
5402 Lisette Ave.
Peoria, IL 61623
(309) 595-3396

Position: Purchasing Agent

Skills:

Purchasing Procedures

Research and study suppliers for best price structure
Reduce or eliminate extravagant lead time
Insure quality of materials purchased
Develop new purchasing systems
Systematize all facets of formal buying program: policies, methods, reporting, files
Centralize purchasing procedures for several plants

Vendor Relations

Establish new vendors to assure competitive pricing
Broaden supply sources
Select and evaluate vendors
Maintain excellent vendor relations
Negotiate vendor changes when necessary

Inventory Control

Reduce inventory investment by substantial amounts
Control stocks as part of cost reduction program
Eliminate duplication of stock in several plants
Establish more efficient reporting system between plants and purchasing office

Supervision

Hire and train staff
Supervise buyers, expediters, clerks
Administer daily operations of 20 people

Employer:

Cannon Industries, Inc., Peoria, IL

—Assistant Purchasing Agent   1978-present
—Buyer and Expediter   1976-1978

Education:

B.S. in Business Administration, University of Oklahoma, Stillwater, 1976

Marketing/Advertising Research
First-job-seeker/recent college graduate
Type of resume: **skill-based**

Glenda Harrington
4582 Pine Cone Lane, Apt. 23
Boulder, CO 80312
(303) 540-1145

Objective: Position in Marketing or Advertising Research

Education:

1983   M.B.A. in Marketing, University of Colorado, Boulder
1979   B.S. in Commerce and Finance, University of Wyoming, Laramie
       cum laude and Dean's List

Concentrated Studies in:

Consumer Behavior   Sales Force Management

Business Law   Calculus

Mass Communications   Economics

Advertising   Statistics

Seminar Topics/Papers:

Effects of environmental protection ethic on advertising strategies of major oil
    companies

Selling the West: family consumer response to advertising campaigns promoting outdoor
    vacations

Social and managerial concepts in mass marketing

Work Experience:

Coors Brewery, Boulder, CO

—administrative assistant to sales manager with responsibilities in billing, inventory
    updating, correspondence and public relations

(Summer 1981)

—sales and management trainee in billing, orders, shipping, and inventory

(Summers 1979-80)

References available on request.

Judson McDonald
5490 Sagebrush Drive
Dallas, Texas 75231
(214) 456-3397

Job Objective: Marketing management position with an international fashion corporation

Areas of Expertise:

Sales Forecasting	Product Development
Customer Relations	Hiring, Training Sales Personnel
Marketing	Territory Layout
Merchandising	Contract Negotiation
Distribution	Sales Meetings
Trade Shows	Business Law

Achievements:

* developed and introduced eight new lines of teenage fashions accounting for $2 million sales annually

* in four-year period, tripled sales volume of declining line of women's summer apparel

* arranged international contracts to distribute and sell line of jeans in Central and South America

* increased market share of a fashion product from 28 to 40 percent in 12-month period

* selected, trained, and directed sales force, many of whom won regional and district honors

* developed highly acclaimed performance evaluation and field training programs still in use after 12 years

Work History:

1979-present	Levco Fashions, Dallas, Texas
1975-1978	Pantalon Fashions, Dallas, Texas

Education:

1974	M.B.A., University of Michigan, Ann Arbor, MI
1971	B.A., Lansing College, Lansing, MI

Military:

1965-1967	United States Navy

References available on request.

Marketing
Production Manager
Second-job-changer
Type of resume: **combination chronological/functional**

Michael Lexa
3549 Jefferson Ave.
St. Louis, MO 63116
(314) 897-3384

Job Target: Production Manager

Employer: Ralston Purina, St. Louis, Missouri 1970-present

Production Manager (1979-82)

—wrote annual marketing strategies and product forecasts; directed staff of 45 in all
phases of marketing, production planning, sales management, advertising, pricing,
profit margin improvement; coordinated research and development of new
promotional concepts; negotiated contracts with outside financial consultants;
selected, trained, and motivated a sales force of 20; successfully increased market
share of top quality grain feed from 24 to 28 percent in nine-month period.

Research Analyst (1974-1979)

—identified and evaluated potential markets for new lines of pet food; monitored sales
trends; collected data on competitors; forecasted annual industry demand for Ralston
products by determining customer needs; determined costs for packaging,
transporting, and distributing products on regional bases.

Sales Representative (1970-1974)

—represented the company as a field sales representative; sold grain, livestock feed,
cereals, and pet foods in the Midwest District; increased sales volume considerably;
acquired new customers and maintained good customer relations.

Education:

M.A. in Marketing 1975
        University of Illinois, Edwardsville
        Funded by Ralston Purina

B.S. in Business Administration 1970
        Sagamuck College, Springfield, Illinois

Personal:

        Born October 5, 1948
        Married
        Willing to relocate

References available upon request.

Alicia Murphy
5838 York Street Apt. 4-R
Toronto, Ontario
(416) 675-2131

CAREER GOAL: Position in advertising department of a clothing manufacturer

SKILLS AND CAPABILITIES:

Create merchandising programs for retail department stores

Design advertising plans by region or state

Conceive and write copy for sales letters, brochures, posters, and counter displays

Work with artists and graphics technicians

Coordinate news releases, photos, and other media announcements

Conduct consumer interviews

Run market surveys, and process and evaluate data

Obtain services for mailing and distribution of samples

Direct couponing programs

Initiate promotion plans for new products

Improve sales of slow-moving merchandise by integrated promotional programs

Create budgets for promotional campaigns

WORK RECORD:

Falcon Industries, Toronto, Ontario
—Promotion Manager, 1978-present

ARV Fashions, Inc., Buffalo, NY
—Assistant Promotion Manager, 1976-1978
—Sales Representative, 1973-1976

EDUCATION:

B.A., Niagara University, Buffalo, NY, 1973

Honors Diploma, Attica High School, Buffalo, NY, 1969

References available on request.

Sales Director (Marketing)
Second-job-seeker
Type of resume: **functional**
Special circumstances: after 18 years with one company, Kent
has been laid off and is now seeking his second job; functional
resume emphasizes steady and consistent promotions; see cover
letter, page 170.

Kent Brandon   4567 Riverview Dr.   Green Hills, AL 35211   (205) 343-4729

Objective: Position in sales/marketing department

Experience:

Marketing/Sales Director
   1977-1983

—responsible for sales administration; territorial layout; hiring, training, motivating sales
   force of 45; product development; sales forecasting; establishment of new markets; in five
   years added eight new area distributors and five key dealerships; increased sales volume
   300 percent.

Regional Sales Manager
   1970-1977

—complete responsibility for sales of all products in 16 states east of Mississippi River;
   represented corporate divisions of company; directed sales force that produced $3
   million in sales annually.

District Sales Manager
   1967-1970

—field sales representative to 11 southeastern states; built up substantial distribution of all
   company brands; added 25 new outlets and increased sales by 200 percent in three years.

Sales Representative
   1965-1967

—sales representative for Mississippi and Alabama; added five new customers; improved
   customer relations.

Employer:

Ornco Glass Corporation, Birmingham, Alabama

Education:

M.A. in Marketing, University of Alabama, Birmingham
   1972

B.A. in History and Literature, Decatur College, Atlanta, GA
   1965

References available on request.

Willing to relocate.

Janet Purcell
9485 Sunrise Blvd. Apt. 5
San Francisco, CA 94121
(415) 798-5693

Career Goal: Reporter/Writer for arts and cultural department of a newspaper

Writer:

* wrote six articles for series "Bay Area Sculptors" for West Coast Arts

* wrote four feature articles for Gallery Today

* wrote and illustrated children's series for Scholastic Enterprises:

    "How to See a Painting," "How to Hear a Poem,"

    "How to Watch a Movie"

* reviewed books and films for Oakland Eagle

Researcher:

* researcher and administrative assistant for Arts Weekly

Editor:

* edited 30 filmstrips for high-school use in fields of art history and architecture for Scholastic Enterprises

Work Experience:

1975 to present	Free-lance Writer
1971 to 1974	Scholastic Enterprises, Oakland, CA
1970 to 1971	Arts Weekly, Inc., San Francisco, CA

Education:

1970	B.A. in Humanities (magna cum laude)
	Regis College, Denver, CO

Willing to relocate on West Coast.

References and writing samples available upon request.

Newspaper
Staff Writer/Researcher
First-job-seeker/ex-military
Type of resume: **skill-based with accomplishment emphasis**

Harold Trunka
939 Dock Road
Portland, Maine 04112
(207) 787-1154

Objective: Staff Writer or Researcher in science department of a newspaper

SKILLS

—research, organize information, simplify complex material, write on technical topics for both lay and professional readers, use computers and word processors, copy-edit, proofread.

EXPERIENCE

—wrote conservation articles for Down East magazine

—associate editor of environmental newsletter directed to Maine State Park and Wildlife Service personnel

—contributor to Overseas, monthly magazine directed to American military personnel in NATO

—wrote technical articles and instructional material for "Field Operations," and handbook on weaponry for field officers in West Germany

Education:

1976   B.A. in Journalism (minor in geography)

Bangor College, Bangor, Maine

Military Service:

1976-1983   United States Army

—stationed in Frankfort, West Germany

Personal:

Born June 4, 1957

Single

Interests: science, geography, wildlife, weaponry, land use, history

References and writing samples available.

Newspaper
Researcher/Staff Writer
First-job-seeker/recent college graduate
Type of resume: **functional**

Jonathon Irving
8493 West Hollow Street
Madison, WI 53715
(608) 931-5593

Objective: Researcher/Staff Writer in news department on a newspaper or magazine

Experience:

* Wrote regular column on political issues for University News; interviewed people in the news; won community service award for on-going series "Reaganomics on the Campus"

1980-1983

* Statistician-writer for "Citizen Alert" pamphlets on crime, pollution, neighborhood renovation, and legal aid services (sponsored by the Green Bay City Council)

Summer 1981

* Researcher and assistant speech writer for Congressman Jake Sternberg, Wisconsin Legislative Assembly Internship, Madison, WI

Feb-April 1981

* Assistant researcher and statistician for CBS opinion poll, Election 1980, Regional Election Headquarters, Milwaukee, WI

Fall 1980

Education:

1983   B.A. in Political Science (minor in journalism)

University of Wisconsin, Madison

Other Work Experience:

waiter, camp counselor, shoe salesman

References and writing samples available on request.

Clerk/Typist
Second-job-seeker
Type of resume: **skill-based**

Eileen McCloskey
457 Bluff Road
Spokane, Washington 99217
(509) 325-6031

Position: Clerk/Typist

Office Skills:

* type—85 wpm

* shorthand—100 wpm

* copy machine

* calculators

* filing systems

* dictaphone

Capabilities:

* typing invoices, contracts and agreements, financial reports,
  business correspondence, insurance forms

* maintaining up-to-date files on customers, subcontractors, suppliers,
  and employees

* providing routine office assistance to co-workers

Employer:

Holowell Construction Corporation

Spokane, Washington

Education:

Cascade High School, Spokane, Washington 1979

Willing to relocate on West Coast.

References available on request.

Cynthia Marlowe
5309 Reading Road
Elkridge, MD 21284
(301) 545-2291 (evenings)

Job Objective: Administrative Assistant

Capabilities:

—supervise office staff: receptionist, typists, filing clerks, messengers
—handle business and social correspondence
—maintain and facilitate business and social calendar
—screen in-coming calls
—receive visitors
—plan itineraries: make travel reservations, book lodgings
—organize preparations for staff and executive meetings
—take notes and prepare minutes of meetings
—prepare and disseminate executive memos
—host and attend public relations events
—in absence of the president, channel mail and phone calls to other executives or secretaries
—purchase office supplies

Work History:

1974-present	Executive Secretary to Dr. Randolph J. Turner, Director, Maryland Heart Institute, Baltimore, MD
1968-1974	Secretary/Receptionist to Dr. Carl Ontkean, Baltimore, MD
1967-1968	Clerk/Typist, Maryland Department of Transportation, Baltimore, MD

Education:

1967	Secretarial Certificate, Tidewater Junior College, Baltimore, MD

Personal:

—born: September 15, 1948
—married, two children
—active in community organizations (Urban League, NAACP)
—interests: sewing, girl scouts, community theater, and dance companies

References available on request.

Secretary
Career-changer
Type of resume: **skill-based/chronological**
Special circumstances: after the death of her husband and a long
career working for major businesses, Regina seeks a more restful
position as a private secretary. See cover letter, p. 176.

Regina Martin
9384 Buckingham Road
Chicago, IL 60611
(312) 563-6039

Objective: Position as private secretary or bookkeeper

Skills:

   Shorthand—120 wpm
   Typing—90 wpm
   Letter Composition
   Office Machines
   Bookkeeping

Experience:

   —handle all standard secretarial duties
   —prepare minutes of business meetings
   —compose letters from minimum of dictated information
   —make travel and lodging reservations
   —maintain daily business and personal calendar
   —supervise other office workers

Work Record:

1972-present   Resorts International, Public Relations Office, Chicago

1965-1972   Holiday Inn, Accounting Department, Memphis, TN

1955-1965   Johnson Manufacturing, Little Rock, AR

1950-1955   Little Rock Gazette, Little Rock, AR

Education:

   Green's Business College, Baton Rouge, LA
   —graduated 1947

References available on request.

Secretary
First-job-seeker/housewife
Type of resume: **skill-based**

Isabel Alfonso
4593 Holly Hills Blvd.
Portland, Oregon 97215
(503) 545-3397

Job Objective: secretarial position in a small office

SKILLS:

—take shorthand 140 wpm

—type 80 wpm

—handle correspondence and telephone messages

—maintain appointment calendar

—compose letters from dictation notes

—operate copy machines, calculator, and word processor

—perform standard bookkeeping procedures: accounts receivable, accounts payable, invoices and vouchers, ledger maintenance, taxes, monthly statements

WORK EXPERIENCE:

1970-1979   St. Rita's Catholic Church, Portland, OR

                 Parish Secretary, part-time

1962-1981   Alfonso Realty, Portland, OR

                 Secretary/Bookkeeper, part-time

REFERENCES:

        Monsignor O'Reilly, St. Rita's, Portland, OR

        Harriet Frances, office manager, Alfonso Realty, Portland, OR

EDUCATION:

        McKinley High School, Salem, OR

        1960, Secretarial Diploma

Secretary
Job-changer
Type of resume: **chronological**

Wanda Latimore
9304 Herring Cove Circle
Jacksonville, FL 32217
(904) 545-3968

Objective: Supervisor of secretarial services in small to medium-sized company

Work History:

1975-present   Holsworth Insurance Group, Jacksonville, FL

Office Manager: supervise office staff of 12; delegate responsibilities; make out work schedules; purchase all supplies; prepare weekly business reports; handle all matters related to personnel, vacations, hiring, training.

1973-1975   Plaza Health Center, Jacksonville, FL

Secretary/Bookkeeper for a group of seven doctors; supervised two full-time and three part-time clerical workers; handled appointments, billing, invoices, purchases; prepared monthly statements.

1969-1973   St. Mary's Hospital, Jacksonville, FL

Hired originally as typist in medical records department and was promoted in one year to supervisor of clerical services; responsible for accurate typing, filing, and maintenance of patients' medical records.

Education:

1968   The Professional Business School, Gainesville, FL

1970   Two courses in medical records, Jacksonville Community College

References:

R.D. Holsworth, Holsworth Realty, Jacksonville, FL

Michael McRae, M.D., Director, Plaza Health Center, Jacksonville, FL

Marcia Dawson, St. Mary's Hospital, Jacksonville, FL

Personal:

Single

Willing to relocate.

Personnel
Second-job-seeker
Type of resume: **skill-based**

Stewart Jackson
7839 Forby Road
Spokane, WA 99214
(509) 343-7947

POSITION: Employee relations coordinator with a West Coast company

PRACTICAL EXPERIENCE IN:

Personnel Management

—study jobs, categorize positions, write job descriptions

—interview prospective applicants

—train personnel in management-by-objectives program

—keep accurate, up-to-date records on all employees

—conduct exit interviews

—provide recommendations and references for former employees

—inform and counsel employees regarding company policies and procedures

—initiate preliminary stages toward settlement of union grievances

Wage and Salary

—conduct salary surveys

—classify jobs within salary ranges

—handle stage 1 of employee grievances

Training

—develop training programs

—organize management seminars for supervisors

—create liaisons with local colleges for special courses

Benefits

—administer two pension programs

—process employee requests under health insurance plan

—develop on-going employee recreation program

Employer: Funkhausen Lumber Corporation, Spokane, WA   1977-present

Education: B.A. in Psychology, Coeur d'Alene College, Idaho   1977

References available on request.

Personnel
Career-changer/ex-teacher
Type of resume: **skill-based**

Cordelia Withers
6590 Jefferson Ave.
Metairie, LA 70013
(504) 445-7837

Career Goal: Administrative position in Department of Human Resources, City of New Orleans

Skills:

Counseling and Career Planning

Interviewing

Administration

Supervision

Performance Evaluation

Policy Interpretation

Recruitment and Promotion

Grievance Settlement

Organization Strategies

Research and Report Writing

Ten Years Practical Experience in:

Student counseling	Student-Faculty Discipline Committee
Freshman orientation	Student ombudsman
Hiring and Retention Committee	Student-Staff Grievance Committee
Faculty Search Committee	Student recruiting

Position:

Associate Professor of Literature and Languages

Tulane University, New Orleans

Education:

Ph.D in Romance Languages, New York University	1972
M.A. in Comparative Literature, St. Louis University	1968
B.A. in English, Windover College, Dodge City, KS	1964

References available on request.

Personnel
First-job-seeker/recent college graduate
Type of resume: **skill-based**

Bart Havelock
9483 Tigerby Road Apt. 36
Houston, Texas 77014
(713) 594-1179

OBJECTIVE: Personnel Interviewer with opportunity for advancement to personnel management

SKILLS:

* Interviewing

* Statistical Analysis

* Report Writing

* Questionnaire Development

* Policy Formulation

* Instructional Procedures

EXPERIENCE:

Interviewing

—research project for senior seminar: The Texas Job Market, 1970-80
  —responsible for interviewing 80 workers (blue collar to executive positions) who have migrated to Texas since 1970, analyzing data, and contributing to final report

Long-range Planning

—student representative on university's long-range planning committee; served on subcommittee dealing with faculty retention and hiring policies

Statistics Analysis

—collected and analyzed statistical data at GOP Houston Headquarters during 1980 presidential election

Free-lance Writing

—"Texas or Bust: The New Settlers in Texas," Texas Today, September, 1983.

EDUCATION:

B.A. in Sociology, Rice University, Houston, 1983

—concentration studies: employee relations, work ethic and American values, industrial psychology

Personnel
Wage and Salary Administrator
Second-job-seeker
Type of resume: **functional**

Kathryn Pisaneschi
659 Roberts Avenue
San Francisco, CA 94121
(415) 735-9285

Job Target: Position in personnel management or salary administration

Experience:

<u>Wage and Salary Specialist</u>   McGraw-Hill Publishing Company
San Francisco, CA (1977-present)

Responsibilities:

* evaluate jobs

* determine job grading system

* conduct performance appraisals with department managers

* maintain employee budget

* determine and justify merit increases and adjustments

* approve job descriptions

* establish salary ranges

* report on vacations, leaves of absence, and sick time

* conduct compensation surveys

* counsel employees

Education:

Bachelor's degree in Psychology and Economics (double major)
University of California, Santa Cruz, 1976

Personnel Management Institute
Berkley University, Summer 1979

Personal:

Born January 8, 1955, Turo Bay, CA
Married
Interests: canoeing, sewing, gourmet cooking

References available upon request.

Kathy Michaels
1498 Middletown Highway Apt. 4-A
Middletown, Kentucky 40215
(502) 659-3316

Job: Photographer

Capabilities:

Photography Skills

* portrait   * nature close-ups

* food photography   * interior decorations

* outdoor scenics   * catalog shootings

Production Skills

* all darkroom procedures   * multiple overlays

* mounting and packaging   * slide production

* flat art   * photo essays

Work Experience:

Assistant Production Manager
A.B. Morris Studios, Louisville, KY
1978-present

Staff Photographer
Tredemont College News, Tredemont Yearbook
1975-1977

Free-lance Photographer
Kentucky Collectibles, Bluegrass Press, Louisville
Simpson Advertising Agency, Louisville

Education: 1977 B.A. in Art, Tredemont College, Louisville, KY

1978 Cumberland Art Institute, Lexington, KY

References and sample work available upon request.

Willing to relocate.

Photographer's Stylist
Career-changer
Type of resume: **functional**
Special circumstances: dates omitted to conceal spotty work record
and series of part-time and seasonal jobs; length of employment
indicated in a few places by number of years

Stephen Brower
482 Coral Lane
St. Petersburg, FL 33742
(813) 365-9385

Job Objective: to work for a photographer who needs an assistant or stylist with a variety of
studio and office talents

Set Designer, Sarasota Little Theater, Sarasota, FL

—designed and constructed sets for five plays per season for four years; included
furnishing props and renting or making costumes

Window Dresser, The Emporium, St. Petersburg, FL

—designed seasonal displays for twelve windows; responsible for materials and staff
of four; worked closely with department heads and promotion director

Antique Dealer, One More Time Antiques, Tampa, FL

—reupholstered and refinished furniture; created window displays; responsible for
some purchasing; also assisted customers in making purchases

Museum Guide/Business Manager, The Rutford House Museum, Tampa, FL

—worked two years as assistant manager/guide for this small Victorian home;
responsibilities included booking tour groups, leading visitors through rooms,
conducting "living history" scenarios (costumes, seasonal decorations, special
events, household chores, celebrations)

Education: University of Florida, St. Petersburg
B.A. in Art and Fashion Design, 1976

Personal Interests: photography, oil painting, antiques, movies

Public Relations
Second-job-seeker
Type of resume: **skill-based**

Thomas Duggan
939 North Shore Drive Apt. 433
Chicago, IL 60613
(312) 353-5592

JOB TARGET: Account Executive for a public relations firm

SKILLS IN PUBLIC RELATIONS MANAGING:

—coordinate public relations activities for five clients

—develop product and service publicity

—secure media time

—buy advertising space

—write, edit, release news items

—arrange company meetings and trade shows

—handle travel arrangements and lodgings

—prepare annual reports

—schedule news conferences

—supervise staff of two writers

—prepare budgets

—design and execute graphic arts displays, logos, etc.

WORK HISTORY:

1978-present	Henricks Public Relations, Inc., Chicago, IL Position: public relations manager	
1977-1978	Michigan Graphics, Inc., Chicago, IL Position: graphics artist	
1976-1977	Tau Kappa Epsilon, National Fraternity, Chicago, IL Position: area representative and recruiter	

EDUCATION:

1977	B.A. in Psychology, Mundelein College, Chicago, IL
1973-1975	Studied at Helman Art Institute, Aurora, IL

References available upon request.

Public Relations
Fund raiser
First-job-seeker/housewife
Type of resume: **combination**

Penny Sanderson
5603 Lucas Blvd.
Omaha, Nebraska 68113
(402) 919-3956

Job Objective: Position as Assistant Fund Raising Administrator at
St. Joseph's Children Hospital

Experience Summary:

Twelve years experience with local community and civic organizations as part-time
and volunteer public relations representative. Responsibilities included fund raising;
writing successful grant proposals; public speaking; telephone contact and personal
visits to major sponsors and benefactors; collecting and assimilating information for
news releases; appearances on local TV and radio programs; writing copy for
promotional programs. Enjoy a congenial, professional relationship with the major
public affairs officers of the local news media.

Work Experience:

Tully Press, Omaha, Nebraska

—advertising assistant to promote publicity and increase subscriptions for
Omaha Magazine (1978-present)

Omaha Suicide and Crisis Intervention Center

—fund raiser, public speaker, and grant proposal writer (1978-present)

Great Plains Fair, Inc., Omaha, Nebraska

—public relations liaison between GPF and 12 major sponsors and supporters
(April-September, 1970-1977)

Girl Scouts Council of Omaha

—assistant coordinator for two annual fund raising drives (1970-1976)

Education:

B.A. in English, University of Missouri, Kansas City, 1963

References available.

Public Relations
Administrative Assistant to Public Relations Director
Career-changer
Type of resume: **skill-based**
Special circumstances: after five years experience as an
administrative assistant to a public relations director, Mary is
applying to a company with an opening in public relations.

Mary Jenkins
4390 Rand Avenue
Haverford, PA 18135
(215) 454-7920

Position: Assistant Director of Public Information

COMMUNICATIONS/PUBLICITY

—prepare news releases; maintain personal media contacts; prepare and edit copy
for brochures, displays, posters; execute advertising strategies; place
advertisements and notices in external organs; collect and edit copy for quarterly
newsletter; prepare and distribute daily in-house newsletter during peak tourist
season; book entertainment; receive and host dignitaries

MEETINGS/TRAVEL

—host and attend seminars and publicity workshops; handle hotel and travel
arrangements for large groups; book convention space; organize staff and
executive meetings

OFFICE ADMINISTRATION

—supervise office staff of six; maintain business and personal calendar; handle
priority phone calls; purchase office supplies; attend to all business and personal
correspondence; prepare periodic reports

SECRETARIAL SKILLS

—typing, dictation, office machinery, bookkeeping, filing

Present Employer:

Heritageland Park, Valley Forge, Pennsylvania
Administrative Assistant to Director of Public Relations (1977-present)
Advertising Assistant (1976-1977)

Education: B.A. in Literature, Temple University, Philadelphia

Willing to relocate.

References available upon request.

Public Relations
First-job-seeker/ex-military person
Type of resume: **functional**

Lawrence Gibberman
2400 Sheridan Ave.
Baltimore, MD 21215
(301) 454-3396

Job Objective: Public Relations Officer for large American corporation with subsidiary
                  companies in Western Europe

Experience:

Assistant Public Affairs Officer

United States Navy, stationed aboard the Oklahoma, Cornua, Italy, 1977-1983

—responsibilities included transportation and briefing arrangements for all foreign

and domestic VIPs; transportation and scheduling of members of the press

visiting command units in the Mediterranean; translation of NATO exercises

at sea; dissemination of information regarding American presence in Europe

to foreign media correspondents and dignitaries; protocol arrangements for

ports of call in Europe and North Africa, including Communist bloc countries;

supervision of official translations of United States information into French

and Italian; editorial director of United States naval newsletters; preparation

of charts, maps, and statistical data; writing, editing, and narrating

documentary films.

Ensign
United States Naval Academy, Annapolis, Maryland, 1973-1977

—specialized course of studies in journalism, psychology, and public relations

Languages: German, French, Italian, Russian

Education:
            1977   Graduated from Annapolis Naval Academy

            1972   Graduated with Honors from Winfield Military Academy, Albany, GA

References available upon request.

Assistant Editor
Second-job-seeker
Type of resume: **chronological**

Penelope Bryant
4920 Blue Ridge Parkway Apt. 4
Roanoke, VA 23289
(703) 696-2580

OBJECTIVE: Assistant Editor for a magazine

1979-present   <u>Teen Years,</u> Blue Ridge Press, Roanoke, VA

Assistant Editor: responsibilities included receiving and evaluating submitted manuscripts for this monthly magazine; participating in selection of manuscripts; working closely with authors, artists, designers; copy editing and rewriting; proofreading at all stages; in addition to work on monthly publications, assisted with editing, rewriting, condensing copy, and designing biennial anthology editions of short stories, articles, and poetry; represented magazine at young adult publishing conferences; conducted workshop on "Violence as Fact and Fiction" (Southeast Association of Young Adult Publishers and Writers, 1980)

1978-1979   <u>CAPS: The Capitol Hill Newsletter,</u> Washington, D.C.

Copy editor: checked completed articles and news items for accuracy before printing each day

Reporter: covered occasional events, wrote copy

Education: 1976   B.A. in Literature, Hollins College, Roanoke, VA
Minor in journalism
Graduated summa cum laude

Foreign Languages:

Fluent in French; reading knowledge of Italian

Interests:

Children's literature, consumer issues, travel, the impact of the new technology on life-styles and values

Willing to relocate.

References available on request.

Copywriter
Second-job-seeker
Type of resume: **chronological with functional emphasis**

Susanna Washburn
259 West 67th St. Apt. 26-F
New York, NY 10062
(212) 656-3952

Objective: Copywriter

Work History:

Dandelion Press, NYC   <u>Staff Copywriter</u>
1978-present

* create and write advertising copy for two book catalogs a year

* research and write book proposals (including sales letter, rationale, table of contents)

* write cover copy

* write captions for illustrations and copy for side bars

* assist with layout and paste-up

* copy-edit accepted manuscripts along with some line editing and rewriting

1976-1978   <u>Free-lance Writer</u>

* aided in scripting three educational films

* commissioned to develop book ideas and draft sales proposals for two book-packaging companies

* placed three articles in a leading women's magazine

* wrote celebrity profiles for theater/film guidebook

* wrote "neighborhood news" column for a weekly newspaper

Education: B.A. in Art and Art History, Brown University 1975

See attached listing of publications and projects.

Writing samples available on request.

Kathryn Buckly
5402 Clearwater Drive
Eau Claire, Wisconsin 54793
(715) 545-8921

Career Goal: editorial position with textbook department of a publishing company

Writer/Editor

* Co-editor of two reading anthologies and author of accompanying workbooks for American Thought and Culture Survey

* Served as editor of 124-page college literary journal appearing three times a year, publishing articles by students and alumni; read, evaluated manuscripts, edited accepted manuscripts; proofread articles at all stages of preparation

* Have published widely in both scholarly and popular journals

* Reviewed books for local newspaper

Textbook Consultant

* Served seven years on Textbook Selection Committee for Division of Liberal Arts

* Made final decision concerning selection and approval of texts used in American Studies program

* Continuously monitored student reactions to textbooks used in each Liberal Arts course by means of questionnaires distributed each semester

Educator

* Headed Department of American Studies (1978-1980); hired faculty, scheduled courses, enrolled students, taught three courses each semester, conducted writing seminars

Education: Ph.D. in American Studies, University of Minnesota, 1972
M.A. in American History, University of Wyoming, 1968
B.A. in English, St. Mary-of-the-Plains, Dodge City, KS, 1966

Employment: Associate Professor of American Studies, Winona College, Eau Claire, Wisconsin, 1975-present

Assistant Professor of History, University of Oregon, Eugene, 1972-1975

Editorial Assistant
First-job-seeker/recent college graduate
Type of resume: **functional**

Charles Woods
396 Palmetto Lane Apt. 4-A
Columbia, S.C. 29263
(803) 565-3189

Job Target: Editorial Assistant

Editorial Experience

—Senior Editor of campus newspaper; made final decisions regarding selection of articles and editorial positions on current issues; edited copy

—Student Editorial Assistant on university literary magazine; proofread and line-edited copy

—Copy Editor for Alumni News

—Researcher/Historian/Copy Editor for university's Centennial Brochure

—Research Assistant for local TV evening news program; responsible for checking accuracy and style of news copy

Related Experience

—Writer/Reporter: wrote weekly editorial column for campus newspaper; carried out investigative reporting and wrote articles relating to campus activities; wrote copy for student handbook committee

—Production Assistant: hired photographers, layout artists, writers; assisted in design and layout of literary magazine and Centennial Brochure; worked in university printshop as typesetter and offset press operator

Education

B.A. in Journalism, South Carolina University, Columbia, SC, 1983

Journalism Scholarship, 1982
Internship Senior Year with WCOL-TV, Columbia

Interests

Politics, conservation, wildlife, poetry, music

References available on request.

Restaurant
Banquet Manager
Career-changer
Type of resume: **skill-based**
Special circumstances: after a long career in restaurant
management, Jeffrey is seeking a managerial position with a hotel.

Jeffrey Littleman
5930 Coral Reef Road
Tallahassee, FL 32314
(904) 495-1139

Position Desired: Banquet Manager for Sheraton Center

FOOD PREPARATION

—planned menus for wide variety of occasions
—supervised all aspects of kitchen activities
—established excellent record as chef
—directed meal preparation for banquets of 25 to 400 people

MANAGEMENT

—ordered all food and drink
—ordered all kitchen and dining room supplies
—established and worked within budget
—oversaw maintenance of equipment and facilities

TRAINING

—personally hired and trained kitchen and dining-room staff
—maintained directory of emergency backup staff
—wrote time-management guidelines for entire staff
—drew up work schedules

PUBLIC RELATIONS

—met with banquet hosts to plan menus
—acted as liaison with special caterers
—maintained excellent relations with unions
—determined number of guests, made parking arrangements

Work History

The Hungry Ox, Tallahassee, FL

—restaurant manager (1972-present)
—assistant manager (1970-1972)

The Sands Hotel and Restaurant

—assistant manager (1966-1969)
—head waiter (1965-1966)

Education: A.S. in food service, Tallahassee Junior College, 1966

Motel Management
Second-job-seeker
Type of resume: **functional**

Fred Striebel
5949 Windswept Bay
Orlando, Florida 32815
(305) 595-3317

Job Objective: Motel Manager

Work History:

<u>Resident Manager</u>   1977-present

—in charge of all bookkeeping, payroll, personnel allocation, public relations, and advertising. Directed an intensive advertising campaign that significantly increased convention and banquet trade. After two years motel returned extra profit and a 50-unit expansion program was begun.

<u>Assistant Manager</u>   1974-1977

—supervised front office, switchboard, housekeeping staff and grounds maintenance crews. Hired and trained all personnel. In charge of all purchasing (excluding restaurant). Coordinated convention and banquet facilities with dining-room manager.

<u>Chief Desk Clerk</u>   1973-1974

—issued keys, distributed mail; handled all registration, reservations and guest billing. Advised housekeeping of arrivals and departures of guests.

Present Employer:

Coral Gables Motel, Orlando, Florida

Education:

Fort Lauderdale Senior High 1966

Military:

United States Marine Corps 1966-1973
Stationed in Vietnam

Personal:

Born May 21, 1948
Married
Interests: hunting, sailing, fishing

References available upon request.

Willing to relocate.

Restaurant Management
First-job-seeker/recent college graduate
Type of resume: **skill-based**

Scott Lambert
465 Huron Drive
Duluth, Minnesota 55831
(218) 897-1136

Job Objective: Assistant Restaurant Manager

Areas of Experience:

FOOD PREPARATION

—planned three meals a day for 300 resident students
—worked as assistant cook in pizza restaurant
—assisted cooks in preparation of three meals a day for 120 children and 40 adults at summer camp

FOOD SERVICE

—supervised kitchen staff of eight
—screened and trained student workers (servers, cashier, cleanup and maintenance crews)
—acted as liaison in disputes between student government association and catering service
—substituted as maitre d' and chief steward at an elegant French restaurant
—catered special banquets of 10 to 100 guests

MANAGEMENT

—ordered all food and drink supplies for college cafeteria
—responsible for payroll, purchasing, and all bookkeeping
—balanced budget

Work Record:

1981-present	Food Service Director at Superior College Great Lakes Food Service, Duluth
1980-1981	Student-Assistant Cafeteria Director Superior College, Duluth
1979-1981 (summers)	Dining Hall Director Camp Winetka, Grand Falls, Minnesota
1978-1979	Cook Gino's Pizza, Duluth
1978	Waiter Les Joies Restaurant, Duluth

Education: B.S. in Business, Superior College, Duluth

References available upon request.

Restaurant Management
Job-changer
Type of resume: **chronological**
Special circumstances: Lucille was thirty when she began working in
restaurants; now older and tired of traveling for Red Lobster, she is
seeking a job back in restaurant management

Lucille Rader
5938 Peach Grove
Atlanta, Georgia 30316
(404) 594-1492

Career: Restaurant Manager

Red Lobster, Inc., Atlanta

1978-present	Consultant	

—traveled as quality control consultant to 200 units in southeastern
region; wrote inspection reports and made recommendations
regarding food, service, hygiene, etc.

1972-1978   Restaurant Manager

—supervised kitchen and dining-room staff at Red Lobster unit in
Atlanta; hired and trained personnel; established work schedules;
managed to lower personnel turnover; responsible for purchasing
all supplies and bookkeeping, including payroll.

Delfino's Italian Restaurant, Savannah, GA

1970-1972   Assistant Manager

—supervised kitchen and dining-room staff; approved menus;
maintained food and wine stocks; planned and coordinated
banquets and private parties for this 25-table restaurant.

The Oasis Room, Sunset Hotel, Savannah, GA

1969-1970   Assistant Manager

—duties and responsibilities similar to above. Planned seasonal theme
menus to attract local customers; assisted in booking weekend
entertainment.

1967-1969   Waitress/Cashier

—began work as waitress and cashier when my second child started
school.

Education: A.A. in Restaurant Management, Tidewater Junior College, 1972

References available on request.

Assistant Boutique Manager
First-job-seeker/housewife
Type of resume: **skill-based.** See cover letter p. 177.

Jeannetta Quigly
2395 Pocono Ave.
Harrisburg, PA 17132
(717) 357-4921

Position: Assistant Boutique Manager

Experience:

SALES

—assist customers in making selections
—handle customer complaints and exchanges
—know when to grant and refuse credit
—design and create window and counter displays
—manage promotional materials and media publicity events

BOOKKEEPING

—maintain ledger
—handle accounts payable and receivable
—process invoices
—balance daily sales receipts with cash register funds
—prepare quarterly statements

FASHIONS

—know major designer lines of women's and men's fashions
—understand principles and aesthetics of fashion design
—have working knowledge of fabric, materials, dyes
—read fashion journals to keep up with current and future trends

Positions Held:

Manager, Junior League Thrift Shop   Harrisburg, PA (1974-1978)

Salesclerk, Frances of Harrisburg   Harrisburg, PA (1978-present)

Salesclerk, The Book Nook   Hershey Mall, PA (1969-1971)

Secretary/Treasurer, Junior League   Harrisburg, PA (1978-1980)

Counselor and Director of Miss Junior Achievement Contest
   Junior Achievement Association, Harrisburg (1981)

Education:
   1966   Penn State
          Bachelor's degree in French Literature

References available on request.

Buyer/Retail
Second-job-seeker
Type of resume: **functional**

Charles Leslie
3958 Eagle Plaza West
Trenton, NJ 08615
(609) 254-3396

Objective: Retail men's clothing buyer in large company with nationwide outlets

Experience:

Buyer in Men's Clothing   Goldstein, Inc., Trenton, NJ

—buy men's fashion lines for four stores; attend trade shows;
coordinate seasonal catalog sales; supervise 12 sales personnel at
main store; prepare quarterly sales reports and forecast sales for
upcoming quarter

(1980-present)

Assistant Buyer in Sportswear

—worked as salesclerk in sporting wear department while being
trained as buyer

(1979-1980)

Salesclerk   Champion Sporting Goods, Trenton, NJ

—regular salesclerk in this popular sporting goods store; eight times
named Salesperson of the Month

(1977-1979)

Education:
    1979-1981   Delaware Community College, Trenton, NJ
                       —night courses in merchandising

    1977   Washington High School, Trenton, NJ

Personal:
    Born August 15, 1959

    Single

    Willing to relocate

References available on request.

Retail Department Manager
Career-changer
Type of resume: **skill-based**
Special circumstances: after a career in selling housewares,
Rupert is seeking a career as buyer for a department store.

Rupert Rivers
3405 Sierra Avenue
Albuquerque, New Mexico 87113
(505) 898-3512

Job Objective: Buyer or Buying Office Representative for large department store

Experienced in:

> name-brand merchandise in housewares
>
> local market in Albuquerque area
>
> forecasting future sales
>
> buying procedures, including regular trade shows
>
> stock ordering
>
> warehousing
>
> inventory control
>
> markdowns
>
> sales promotions

Achievements in Houseware Merchandising:

> increased sales volume for housewares department from $300,000 in 1978
> to $500,000 in 1980
>
> consistently earned higher-percent increases in housewares than any
> other store in 1981-1982

Positions Held:

Manager, Housewares Department   Hagerman Department Stores
                                        Albuquerque, NM (1974-present)

Assistant Buyer/Salesclerk   Handy Man, Cactus Plaza Mall
                                        Albuquerque, NM (1970-1974)

Education:

1976   University of New Mexico, Continuing Education Division
       Seminars in Retail Merchandising and Advertising

1970   Randolph High School
       Albuquerque, NM

References available upon request.

Salesclerk
Second-job-seeker
Type of resume: **skill-based/chronological combination**

Mary Elsworth
6530 Freeport Drive
Manchester, NH 03225
(603) 716-3395

Objective: Salesclerk with possibility of promotion to Department Manager or Buyer

Summary: Six years as Salesclerk, fully trained in

SALES

STOCK

WAREHOUSING

REORDERING

ACCOUNTING

CUSTOMER SERVICE

Specific Experience:

Scruggs, Hinckley, and Taylor Department Stores, Manchester, NH   1978-present

—six-month training program in all areas listed above

—three and a half years as salesclerk in children's clothing, toys, lawn and garden departments

—acting department manager for three months during regular manager's absence (maternity leave)

—assisted in designing and executing department and counter promotional displays

Sears Roebuck and Company, Manchester, NH   1976-1978

—part-time salesclerk during busy shopping seasons

Education:

Madison Senior High School, Portsmouth, NH   1978

Personal:

Born March 16, 1962

Married

Health good

References available on request.

Malcolm Fiedler
8394 Buena Vista Blvd.
San Diego, CA 92115
(714) 969-3386

Position: Promotion Manager for a sporting/athletic-goods manufacturer

SKILLS:

Sales	Trade Shows
Sales Training and Supervision	Territory Layout
Customer Service	Pricing
Complaint Settlement	Distributions
Demonstrations	Public Relations

HIGHLIGHTS AS DISTRICT SALES MANAGER:

—ranked number 1 salesman for last four years

—sold $6 million per annum

—established new territory; hired and trained new sales representative; set up three new distributors

—built and maintained excellent, loyal relationship between customers and company

—conducted demonstration seminars on new products for regular customers

WORK HISTORY:

Pacific Marine Supplies, Inc., San Diego, CA
—commercial and recreational boating/fishing equipment

—District Sales Manager   1979-present

—Sales Representative   1976-1979

Aramas Athletic Equipment, San Francisco, CA

—Sales Representative   1974-1976

EDUCATION:

B.A. in Sociology, Hayward College, Hayward, CA 1974

References available on request.

Sales representative
Second-job-seeker
Type of resume: **functional**

George F. Backer
3694 Kellogg Ave. Apt. 2-A
Indianapolis, IN 46213
(317) 294-3396 (Evenings)

JOB TARGET: Sales Representative

Current Position:

Sales Representative   Hartman Industries, Indianapolis   1979-present
                            —office furniture and supplies

* developed a new territory in the Muncie-Anderson area

* identified and obtained new customers among wholesalers, retailers, and private businesses

* established personal contacts with customers

* created and maintained excellent customer relations and enhanced company image

* researched and maintained up-to-date knowledge of competitive products and their current outlets

* devised innovative methods of increasing sales

* added 28 new accounts in first two years

* increased sales by 15 percent per annum in Indianapolis Region

Education:

        1979   Versailles Community College, Indianapolis
                Major: Consumer Affairs

        1977   Greenwood High School, Greenwood, IN
                Major: Physical Education

Personal:
        Born April 3, 1959

        Single

        Interests: sports, outdoor activities, woodworking

Willing to relocate.

References available on request.

Sales
First-job-seeker/recent college graduate
Type of resume: **skill-based**

Richard Altman
4503 Saturn Road
Durham, NC 27719
(919) 746-5302

Job Objective: Sales Representative for nationwide manufacturer or customer service
organization

Experience:

Over-the-counter Sales

—salesclerk in busy neighborhood hardware store; handled purchase orders for

stock; customer complaints; returns; credit; billing

Deliveries/Sales

—delivery-salesman for Hostess Bakery; covered stores and restaurants in

Durham area; processed purchase orders on visits and by phone; set up

displays in stores

Fund Raising

—chairman of Tar River Biology Project; raised $3000 by calling on local

businesses in the Portsmouth Area; established 75 contacts by phone calls

and personal visits; supervised five fund raising assistants

Employers:

Altman Hardware, Durham NC
—family-owned store; worked part-time through high school and summers during
college

Hostess Bakery, Portsmouth, Virginia
—delivery-salesman, 1981-1983

Education:

B.A. in Biology, Varina College, Portsmouth, VA, 1983
—minor in Accounting

Willing to relocate.

References available upon request.

Social Worker
Second-job-seeker
Type of resume: **functional**

Jack Onder
5405 Mount Helen Ave.
Wichita, Kansas 67215
(316) 405-1169

Objective: Position in Family Counseling with a county mental health center

Caseworker   Department of Social Services   1978-present
                              Wichita, Kansas

—carried regular caseload of 30 to 40

—interviewed families applying for financial aid, ADC, food stamps

—visited homes

—determined type of assistance for which applicants qualified

—located jobs for clients by contacting community agencies

—wrote detailed reports with recommendations

—provided training jobs for clients through referrals to local agencies and training centers

—referred serious cases for psychiatric help

—involved in program development to establish summer job and recreational programs
  for teenagers

—acted as liaison with six summer camps that sponsored camperships for needy children

—spoke at high schools, civic organizations, and public meetings on the plight of the needy

—trained college interns in interviewing and home visiting

Education:

    Master's degree in Social Work   Wichita State University   1978

    Bachelor's degree in History   Topeka College, Topeka, KS   1975

Professional Organizations:

    National Association of Social Workers
    Kansas Correctional Association
    American Camping Association

Personal:

    Born June 9, 1954
    Single

References available on request.

Social Worker
First-job-seeker
Type of resume: **chronological**
Special circumstances: since she has done so much volunteer
work, Carola uses a chronological resume.

Carola Bergan   5603 Edwards Ave.   Los Angeles, California 90014   (213) 467-3968

Objective: part-time Counselor with Los Angeles Juvenile Correction Center or any social
welfare agency dealing with delinquent or homeless girls

Experience:

Suicide and Crisis Intervention Center, Los Angeles   (1978-present)

—worked as telephone counselor for three years; promoted to assistant manager of
Center; trained new volunteers; lectured to civic groups and high schools about
depression, suicide, and the Center's work; visited referral agencies and professional
backup staff for the Center; assisted in yearly fund raising events.

Women's Center of Greater Los Angeles   (1976-1981)

—volunteer counselor and interviewer; made referrals to psychiatric staff; led group
sessions and one-on-one sessions; served as group facilitator in some therapy sessions;
specialized in counseling women recently divorced or going through the divorce process.

Camp Borrego, Mountain Spring, CA   (1976-1980)

—interviewed and home-visited families referred to Camp Borrego; this final screening of
children referred to summer camp took place from April to June each year; wrote report
and verified home, family, and personal problems described by referral agencies.

Claremont College, Claremont, CA   (1973-1975)

—stayed on at undergraduate college as assistant manager for woman's housing; reported
directly to Dean of Women; counseled students; referred problems to appropriate college
administrators or physicians and psychiatrists; spent great amount of time dealing with
problems and questions related to sexuality, birth control, relationships, etc.

Education:

20 Graduate Hours in Social Work   (1975-present)
San Bernardino State College
San Bernardino, CA

B.A. Psychology   (1969-1973)
Claremont College
Claremont, CA

References available on request.

Betsy Coleman   2943 Xenia Road   Xenia, Ohio 45321   (513) 565-1139

Career Goal: Public Relations Director for human service agency

Public Speaker

* lecture to school and civic groups about suicide, drug abuse, family problems

* present slide and tape shows on mental health topics

* conduct question and answer sessions on problems of mental health

* serve on discussion panels

* appear on local TV talk shows

Fund Raiser

* chair yearly fund raising drive for mental health center

* create and supervise seasonal fund raising projects for specific mental health programs

* hosted open houses at center every spring for eight years

Writer

* wrote weekly column "Your Mental Health" for Wilmington Gazette

* wrote copy and edited Mental Health in Central Ohio, a monthly newsletter for mental health agencies

* wrote copy for radio announcements and newspaper ads informing public of services offered by the mental health center

* developed and wrote five series of pamphlets on alcoholism, drug abuse, unemployment, death, and divorce (published by Buckeye Press, Columbus, OH)

Agency Representative

* represented mental health center at local and statewide public events

* sent as representative to professional conferences nationwide

* appeared before legislative bodies to report on fiscal needs of mental health agencies in Ohio

Education: M.S.W., Texas State University, Austin   1964
             B.A. in Sociology, Williams College, Williamstown, MS   1961

Present Employer: Wilmington Mental Health Center   1969-present
                     Wilmington, OH

References available on request.

Social Worker
First-job-seeker/recent college graduate
Type of resume: **combination**

Nathan Dark Cloud
3465 Abondale Drive
Boulder, CO 80312
(303) 540-3317

Objective: Position with a welfare agency in the Bureau of Indian Affairs

Education: M.S.W., University of Colorado, Boulder, 1983
             B.A., English and History, University of Colorado, Boulder, 1978

Classroom Experience:

Theory of Social Work	Abnormal Psychology
Social Welfare Systems	Introduction to Sociology
Principles of Sociology	History of Social Welfare
Urban Social Problems	Statistics
Case Analysis	Principles of Economics
Introduction to Psychology	American Indian History (20th Century)

Master's Thesis: "Adjustment Problems of Former Members Returning to
                   Red Wing Reservation from Urban Environments"

Field Experience:

counselor, St. Paul's Home for Boys	1980-1981
interviewer/statistician, U.S. Census Bureau	1979
home visitor, Denver Narcotics Rehabilitation	1978-1979
president, Community Action Club, U. of C.	1978-1979
volunteer, Denver Youth Center, Downtown Branch	1976-1978

Publications:

"I Return, I Stay: A Lakota's Reasons for Returning to His Reservation,"
Journal of the Plains, Summer, 1982.

"Where Do They Sleep?: A Look at Denver's Homeless Citizens,"
Denver Magazine, September, 1980.

"Juvenile Homes: Are They Really Homes?" Rocky Mountain News Magazine,
December 3, 1979.

References available on request.

Teacher
College
Second-job-seeker
Type of resume: **functional**

Carter Rockwell
6520 Wanda Ave.
Seattle, WA 98157
(206) 791-4413

Professional Experience

Teacher:

—taught courses in American History and Literature; conducted senior seminars for American Studies majors; coordinated degree program for American Studies majors; selected textbooks; chaired Humanities Interdisciplinary Committee.

Writer:

—published articles on American thought and culture in professional journals; reviewed books for Seattle Times; wrote narration for educational video program on history of the Northwest Territory; delivered papers at major national conferences on topics such as ecology, land use, images of the West in popular culture, American literature.

Consultant:

—served as participant and consultant in three living history programs for Washington Committee on the Humanities; hired as research consultant for 15-month study on economic development and human values funded by National Endowment for the Humanities and Seattle County Government.

Present Position

Assistant Professor of American Studies   1977-present
Columbia College, Seattle

Education

Ph.D. in American Studies, 1978
University of Wyoming, Cheyenne

M.A. in Literature, 1975
Springfield College, Illinois

B.A. in Humanities, 1972
St. Louis University, MO

See attached list of publications/References available upon request.

George L. Sayer
4523 West Main Street
Cape Girardeau, MO 63745
(314) 343-8218

JOB TARGET: Researcher/technical writer for magazine devoted to the environmental sciences

AREAS OF KNOWLEDGE:

Biology	Ecology
Chemistry	Biotic Land Communities
Agricultural Science	Zoology
Economics	Entomology

WORK EXPERIENCE:

1972-present   Professor of Earth Sciences
University of Missouri, School of Agriculture
Cape Girardeau, Missouri
Courses taught: livestock breeding, plant fertilization, industrial pollutants, pest control, crop improvement, economics

1978-present   Director, SEMO Institute on Environmental Problems
—a four-state program dedicated to improving land productivity and maintaining ecological health in a rapidly changing economic environment

MOST RECENT PUBLICATIONS INCLUDE:

"The Green Revolution in the 21st Century," American Farmer, September, 1979.

"Effects of Delta Steel on Southeast Missouri: A Fifteen-year Study," U.S. Journal of Agriculture, Winter, 1979.

"Missouri's Cave: Resources or Recreation?" Missouri Conservationist, Summer, 1980.

"The Missouri Bootheel and the New Deal: 25 Years Later," report prepared for USDA and published in Journal of American Life, Winter, 1982.

EDUCATION:

Ph.D. in Biology, Stanford University

M.A. in Life Sciences, UCLA

B.A. in History of Science, UCLA

Teacher
Grade school
Second-job-seeker
Type of resume: **functional**

John Fable
3579 Raymond Ave. Apt. 5
Philadelphia, PA 19145
(215) 623-5599

Career Goal: Teaching position in Philadelphia High School while obtaining a Master's
degree in English

Experience: St. Brigit's Grade School, Philadelphia   1978-present

TEACHER

* taught math and science, grades seven and eight
* coordinated upper-grades math program
* taught advanced reading and literature
* tutored eighth graders for high-school entrance exams
* awarded released time for developing remedial math program

MODERATOR

* supervised St. Jude's "Marathon"
* implemented and moderated Safety Patrol Squad
* directed winter pageants and spring musicals
* organized and ran all-school spelling bee

COUNSELOR

* counseled eighth-grade students regarding high-school selection
* acted as assistant principal for disciplinary procedures
* coordinated parent-teacher counseling nights

Education:

1978 B.A. in Education, Temple University, Philadelphia
Minor in English and Math
Dean's List senior year

1974 The Jefferson Elementary Academy, Philadelphia

Member:

National Catholic Educators of America
National Education Association

References available upon request.

Teacher
High School
First-job-seeker/recent college graduate
Type of resume: **combination**

Cynthia Maguire
4390 Stratford Avenue
Louisville, Kentucky 40234
(502) 771-4590

Goal: Teacher of French or Spanish

EXPERIENCE

Education

B.A. in Secondary Education; minor: French and Spanish

Bellarmine College, Louisville, Kentucky, 1983

Courses

History of Education	French (beginning through advanced)
Principles of Education	Spanish (beginning through advanced)
Principles of Secondary Education	Comparative Literature
Special Education	20th Century French and Spanish Literature
Career Counseling	Secondary Administration

Student Teaching

Melville High School, Louisville, KY

—taught First-year Spanish (two sections), fall semester, 1982

—hired part-time to teach Advanced French Literature, Spring, 1983

—served as assistant director in Spring musical, Brigadoon

Travel

Exchange student in Paris, sophomore year, 1979-1980

—traveled extensively in France, Spain, Italy

Extracurricular Activities

Vice-president, Student Government Association

President, French Club

Women's Volleyball Team

Student Representative, Presidential Search Committee

References available upon request.

TV/Radio
Announcer
First-job-seeker/recent college graduate
Type of resume: **functional**

David Rengel
3057 Millerton Ave. Apt. 24
Cincinnati, Ohio 45218
(513) 215-3318

Job Objective: Announcer for TV or radio station

Experience:

* ANNOUNCER

   —staff announcer at WHOH-TV; introduced programs, special guests; occasionally sent
   with news team for on-spot reporting; did voiceovers for commercials and promotional
   spots; midnight DJ at WQRT-FM.

* SCRIPTWRITER

   —wrote copy for news show; assisted in creating scripts for commercials and weather
   stories; rewrote promotional copy.

* PROGRAMMER

   —experience in selecting programs; arranging schedules; auditioning actors, announcers,
   entertainers; assigning personnel for special programs.

* CAMERAMAN

   —served with on-location camera crew for two children's documentaries: "The Park
   Poets" (summer 1979) and award-winning "Zoo Babies" (spring 1980).

Employers:

WHOH-TV, College Internship	January-May 1981
University Radio Station, Announcer/DJ	1980-1982
River City Film Studios, Special Assistant	1980-1981
WQRT-FM, DJ	September 1982-present

Education:

   B.A. in Broadcast Journalism, University of Cincinnati, 1983

References available on request.

Writing and programming samples also available.

Franny Adams
7839 Rhodes Ave. Apt. 31
Chicago, IL 60614
(312) 898-1145

JOB OBJECTIVE: Program Director

WORK HISTORY:

1970-present   WLAK-TV, Chicago, IL

—hired as <u>Assistant Program Director</u> in charge of daytime scheduling;
supervised staff of twenty; responsible for all programs, commercials,
public affairs announcements, and newscasts; in the last five years,
station's daytime ratings have moved up dramatically.

1962-1970   WXIT-TV, Peoria, IL

—originally hired as <u>continuity writer.</u> In less than a year offered position
as <u>promotion writer</u> in charge of logging all 30-second and 60-second
promotional spots; rewrote copy; screened and processed trailers, tapes,
slides; edited tapes for desired length. Promoted to <u>public affairs director</u>
(1965-1970); supervised staff of five; created special programs such as
morning talk show and served as host/narrator on weekend panel
discussion featuring topics of local interest; <u>director of editorials</u>
(1968-1970).

EDUCATION:

1980   M.A. in Mass Communications, University of Chicago, IL

1962   B.A. in Broadcasting, Bradley University, Peoria, IL

Willing to relocate.

Writing and programming samples available on request.

References available.

TV/Radio
Traffic Director
Second-job-seeker
Type of resume: **chronological/functional**

Derick Gentry
6408 Myrlette Court
Boise, Idaho 83714
(208) 646-3395

Job Objective: Traffic Director

Work History:

WBOI-TV, Boise, Idaho

Assistant Traffic Director   10/80 to present

—in charge of creating TV log, establishing sales availabilities, pulling and
distributing teletype information, acting as chief liaison between syndicator of
taped programs and station; received, screened, and processed all tapes and films
for future use; ordered films and shows to coincide with scheduled play dates.

Assistant to the Traffic Director   1/79 to 9/80

—filed and updated TV logs; maintained traffic boards; received and processed
requests for public affairs announcements; prepared advanced program
information for local TV listings.

Special Assistant to Program Director   7/78 to 12/78

—supervised program scheduling; maintained updated log; distributed
supplementary materials for all classroom/course shows; coordinated public
service spots.

Education:

1978   B.A. in English, minor in communication arts

Ketchum College, Boise

Personal:

Born August 30, 1956

Married

Willing to relocate.

References available upon request.

PART III

Cover Letters
That Work

THE IMPORTANT RULES FOR WRITING YOUR LETTER

Never send a resume without a cover letter to introduce you and your resume to your potential employer. Even though it contains all the vital information regarding your work experience and qualifications for the job, a resume is still a rather informal, cold document, and not unlike hundreds of others an employer might receive. The cover letter is warmer, more personal, and is intended to interest the employer in *you* as the unique individual who wrote this particular resume. It is also addressed to a particular person, as your resume is not, and even the busiest employer will most likely read a letter carefully, whereas a resume by itself may get only a cursory skimming.

Here are the cardinal rules regarding the form and content of a cover letter.

1. Always address the cover letter to a specific person if possible. For a small company or business, address it directly to the president or owner. For larger companies, send it to the vice-president or director of the department in which you wish to work. For lower-level clerical jobs, the personnel director will suffice. But do not hesitate to aim high. The top executives of large companies usually have their mail screened anyway so it will not be an annoyance to them, and it is better to have your letter and resume sent down from the top to the appropriate department than to start low (at the personnel department) where it might be filed for future reference and never reach the supervisor who would hire you.

If you do not know the name and title of the person you should send your letter and resume to, call the company and ask for the name, the spelling, the title, department, and address. You need not tell the switchboard operator or secretary the exact reason for your inquiry. Simply state that you have some information to send the particular person. Then address both the envelope and salutation of the letter to that person.

Use a title in the salutation, such as, Mr., Mrs., Ms., Professor, Doctor, etc. Only if you have been previously introduced to the person you are writing to and feel that you are on a first-name basis should you omit the formal title-plus-last-name salutation. If it is impossible to learn the name of the person to send your resume to (such as in answering a job ad in the newspaper), a simple "Dear Sir or Madam" is proper.

2. The first few sentences should be carefully thought out and well written. You want to achieve several things in the first few lines. First, you must grab the employer's attention. Second, you should state very clearly why you are writing this letter, that is, to introduce yourself and your resume. Third, you should indicate your interest in the particular company in such a way that the reader realizes you are familiar with the company and its line of work. If you know there is an opening in your field, say that you do and that it is one for which you are applying. It is a good idea to say something praiseworthy about the company. You might mention its fine reputation or that you have always admired its products or the work it does or the service it performs in the community. If you know someone who works there, you can artfully drop his or her name, suggesting that it was through this employee that you learned about the company or the opening. The point behind all this is to let the employer know that you've "done your

homework'' and are not applying blindly to an unknown company.

3. The next two or three paragraphs should highlight important qualifications about yourself. These may include pertinent facts not on your resume as well as two or three outstanding qualifications cited on the resume itself. You may want to indicate the number of years you have been in the business, the wide background of experience you would bring to the new company, or pinpoint some educational or training experience you have had that would be valuable to your new employer.

The important point is to sell yourself, to create the impression that you would make a valuable contribution to the company or department. Be bold but not egotistical in your phrasing. Be assertive and assured of yourself without sounding pushy or too aggressive. Do not make statements that are not substantiated by the resume or that you could not prove in an interview. Without being overly cute or folksy, you should let your best personality traits shine through the letter.

4. Use the jargon of your profession. Let the reader know you understand and can handle the phrases and terms of the business. But don't go overboard and make your letter sound like a dull, technical memo rather than a personal letter.

5. If your resume indicates that you are currently unemployed, your cover letter should suggest why that is so. Obviously you do not want to say, ''I was axed!'' If indeed you were fired, you should phrase it more favorably to yourself. ''My position was eliminated due to fiscal cutbacks'' or ''organizational restructuring.'' ''I left the company because there was no further possibility of advancement.''

Other valid reasons for leaving (or having left) might include: ''a desire for more challenging work,'' ''to seek a job with greater growth potential,'' ''the current position does not allow me to utilize all my skills and abilities.'' Equally valid is the reason that you require a salary increase (perhaps because of a growing family) that would not be possible with your current company. Another acceptable reason is to relocate to another part of the country because of a spouse's career change or to be near family after the death of a spouse.

You need not mention your reason for leaving a job in a cover letter, of course, but be prepared to have the question asked you in an interview.

Most of all, do not be negative or overly critical of your former employers. If you have had personality clashes or policy differences with them, forgo the desire to write deprecatingly about them. You do not want to suggest in a letter that you cannot get along with your supervisors. Even should the subject come up in an interview, tread carefully and do not dwell on the problem or convey the impression that you resent authority.

6. A cover letter is the proper place to bring up a physical disability or handicap. It is a good idea to alert potential employers to the fact that you are in a wheelchair or are deaf and read lips before they meet you. Again, be positive and matter-of-fact about it, indicating that you can live and work with it and it has not interfered in the past with the type of work you do.

7. The last paragraph of a cover letter should mention your availability and your desire to have a personal interview. Be assertive here. Do not beg or sound subservient. State that you expect to hear from them and that you would like to arrange a time to get together. Be blunt and close the deal: ask for an interview. In taking this approach, you make it natural to follow up with a phone call in ten to fourteen days if you have not heard from them.

To sum up:

1. Be personal but professional.
2. Highlight a few of your outstanding qualifications.
3. Show a sincere interest and knowledge of the company or business.
4. Use the professional jargon of the trade.
5. Do not be egotistical. Don't exaggerate your good qualities. But don't be fawning or begging.
6. Ask for an interview.
7. Be brief. A *one-page* cover letter is enough.
8. Follow one of the professional formats for a business letter. Read all of the following examples to get ideas.

4593 Fremont Avenue
Kansas City, MO 64115

October 6, 1983

Dr. Graham Roberts
Director
Muehlbaum Health Institute
4930 Plaza Avenue
Kansas City, MO 64123

Dear Dr. Roberts:

I am sending you my resume in the hope that my experience and background may be of interest to you and the Health Institute. As you can see, I created the medical records department at the Colorado Heart Institute and have served as chief administrator of it since 1972. I would still be there today, but resigned to accompany my husband to Kansas City where he has been transferred.

I realize you already have a medical records staff. In fact, I have had professional dealings with Helen Kane over the years. My career goal, I know, must remain general at this point, but I love the health care field and would be most happy to discuss with you possibilities that might arise in which I could be of use to the Institute.

If my background seems valuable to you, I would enjoy hearing from you regarding a possible position.

Sincerely yours,

Madelyn Owen

(See accompanying resume page 88.)

1593 Kenneth Drive
Santa Cruz, CA 95011

June 17, 1983

Joanna Cutter
Vice-President
First National Bank
112 South Elm Street
Santa Cruz, CA 95014

Dear Ms. Cutter:

I am applying for a position as bank teller and can bring to the job five years experience in several California banks.

My length of employment with each bank has been somewhat short due to the fact that my former husband's career kept us on the move quite frequently. But I am a reliable and trustworthy teller, as my references, I am certain, will verify.

I am seeking full-time employment, but I would be happy to accept a part-time position, if one is available, while waiting for a permanent spot to open up.

I would welcome an opportunity to meet with you and fill out an application.

Thank you.

Sincerely yours,

Marjorie Tracy

(See accompanying resume page 59.)

4928 Chartres Street
New Orleans, LA 70114

May 1, 1983

Jane P. Gambel
New Orleans Public Library
3416 Canal Street
New Orleans, LA 70122

Dear Ms. Gambel:

I am writing for a position as an assistant librarian in the New Orleans Public Library System.

I am completing my Master's degree in Library Science and will be available to begin full-time work at the end of this month. My experience outside the classroom involved a year's internship in the Children's Department of the Metairie Branch where I learned, in addition to the general duties of a librarian, the particular needs of specialized departments and patrons, in this case children. I would like to continue working with younger patrons if such a position is open.

You can see from my educational background that I have been trained in the various aspects of general library and reference work, and I am willing to begin full-time employment in any department in any branch.

I would appreciate hearing from you to arrange a meeting where we might talk over your current needs.

Thank you. And looking forward to meeting you.

Sincerely yours,

Joyce Langdon

(See accompanying resume page 106.)

4567 Riverview Drive
Green Hills, AL 35211

November 19, 1983

Jerome Wilkerson
Marketing Director
Birmingham Industries
4531 Industrial Drive
Birmingham, AL 35218

Dear Mr. Wilkerson:

I am applying for a position in sales/marketing with your company because I believe that my experience as a sales manager and sales director will be of value to you.

My working career has been with Ornco Glass of Birmingham which as you may know has transferred several major departments, including marketing, to their New York headquarters. Wishing to remain here where my family and social ties are, I resigned rather than be moved. I have three daughters in school and am active in several civic and church organizations.

I enjoy sales very much, and as you can see on my resume, I have been quite successful in promoting products and establishing new markets. Sales volume has consistently increased under my management.

I realize you may not have an opening for a sales director, but I am willing to enter at any managerial level where I could contribute my skill and knowledge to your sales force.

I will be in the vicinity of your offices next week. Could we arrange an interview time?

Thank you for your consideration.

Sincerely yours,

Kent Brandon

(See accompanying resume page 117.)

549 Diana Street
Nashville, TN 37218

December 9, 1983

Hilda Campbell
Director of Nursing Services
Baptist Hospital
2151 West End Blvd.
Nashville, TN 37213

Dear Mrs. Campbell:

I am writing you to inquire about your nursing needs at Baptist Hospital. As you can see from my resume, my nursing experience goes back a long way and has had several challenging episodes, notably overseas and as director of nursing services at a major teaching hospital in the South.

I retired from professional, full-time nursing in 1965 to care for my husband, who was stricken with Parkinson's disease. After his death, I continued to work part-time at the University of Tennessee Medical School Hospital, so I have kept up with the many latest developments in the profession. Now I would like to re-enter nursing full-time and am most willing to take a staff job if there are no supervisory positions open.

I would like to speak further with you about how I might contribute my experience to Baptist.

Looking forward to hearing from you, I am

Sincerely yours,

Rosemary Furlong

(See accompanying resume page 89.)

478 Delta Avenue
Hattiesburg, MS 39416

October 12, 1983

John L. Ludman
Director of Research
Gulf Coast Laboratories
Biloxi, Mississippi 39123

Dear Mr. Ludman:

I am writing in response to your ad announcing a job opening in Gulf Coast Laboratories.

My experience in telephonic communications began in the Air Force where I was trained as a radio repairman and soon promoted to senior level. Eventually I was in charge of training new repair personnel. During these years I encountered many technical and logistical problems to be solved and in doing so decided that I both enjoyed the work and had a natural talent for it. After leaving the Air Force I worked for Bell Telephone and continued my education in electronic communications, always hoping that some day I would have the opportunity to be part of the research end of the field.

I would like to meet with you and talk over the details and responsibilities of the job you are advertising. Could we arrange an interview?

Sincerely yours,

Lowell Sweeney

(See accompanying resume page 63.)

3954 Sunset Avenue
Carol City, Florida 33015

March 15, 1983

Percy Randall
Marina Associates
4590 Waterfront Blvd.
Miami, Florida 33119

Dear Mr. Randall:

Jeff Peters at the Coral Gables Country Club suggested I contact you about the opening in your bookkeeping department at Marina Associates. I have worked for Jeff over the last four summers as a clerk and special assistant during the busy vacation season.

As you can see from my resume, I will be graduating in the spring of 1982 with a degree in business and four years of various bookkeeping experiences behind me. I have been fortunate to have held on to part-time jobs throughout my college years, jobs which allowed me to practice the business skills I was studying in class.

Marina Associates is the type of large, dynamic enterprise in the Miami area that I would like to work for. I was happy to hear of the opening.

I would appreciate the opportunity to meet with you. I live in the general vicinity of Marina Associates and could come by for an interview at your convenience.

Thank you for your consideration.

Sincerely yours,

John Travers

(See accompanying resume page 60.)

3496 Harbert Avenue
Grand Rapids, MI 49511

April 26, 1983

Roger Q. Markham
Empire Construction
3495 Main Street
Grand Rapids, MI 40521

Dear Mr. Markham:

I am writing you about the possibility of joining your company as a carpentry supervisor. I have had fifteen years of construction experience as a carpenter and as president of my own company.

In 1976 Bill Sloan and I merged our companies and together ran a very profitable business until the serious downturn in the economy and Bill's unexpected death in 1980. Together these two events impressed upon me the difficulties of operating a small subcontracting business alone, and I dissolved the company in 1981.

As you probably know from your own experience in the Grand Rapids community, I have been involved with and responsible for some of the major construction projects completed in recent years. I have listed several on my resume.

I know your company has been contracted to begin several important projects within the year, and I would like very much to be part of the team. I would bring to your own company a wide range of supervisory skills and construction know-how.

I will look forward to hearing from you and discussing these matters further.

Sincerely yours,

John Wade

(See accompanying resume page 71.)

5039 Peachtree Street
Macon, Georgia 31244

September 21, 1983

Thomas Wagner, M.D.
Director, The Wagner Clinic
3503 Jackson Avenue
Atlanta, Georgia 30315

Dear Dr. Wagner:

I am applying for a position as rehabilitation therapist with your clinic.

As my resume shows, I have been involved in almost every dimension of physical therapy, and as my patients will attest, I am easy to work with and my treatments produce results. I have been deaf since high school, but I read lips well enough that many people do not realize that I cannot hear until I tell them. In some ways, I believe that my own handicap inspires my patients to work and overcome their own.

I have enjoyed working at Macon General Hospital, but I am moving and would like a job closer to Atlanta.

I will be in your area next month and would appreciate an interview. Either write me at the above address or telephone after 5:00 when my roommate is home.

Thank you for your kind consideration.

Sincerely yours,

Gladys Greene

(See accompanying resume page 93.)

9384 Buckingham Road
Chicago, IL 60611

August 30, 1983

Dear Sir or Madam:

I am answering your ad in the Chicago Tribune for a private secretary.

I have been a secretary for several major companies since 1955 and am well acquainted with the numerous daily tasks required of a secretary and bookkeeper. I enjoy the work, but am looking for a quieter pace than one generally finds in business.

I would bring to the position a keen eye for detail, a consistently professional attitude, and a reliability to meet deadlines and remember appointments. I am also willing to work flexible hours, evenings and weekends when necessary.

I hope to hear from you.

Sincerely yours,

Regina Martin

(See accompanying resume page 123.)

2395 Pocono Avenue
Harrisburg, PA 17132

January 12, 1983

Robert Newman
Dandelion Associates
12 The Randolph Building
Harrisburg, PA 17144

Dear Mr. Newman:

I am applying for a managerial position in the Dandelion Shoppe that will be opening in the new Liberty Mall next spring.

My experience over the last fourteen years has involved me in various aspects of retail work: sales, bookkeeping, fashions, promotional ideas, as well as managing the Junior League Thrift Shop. I enjoy retail sales in women's apparel and have made it a kind of hobby over the years: reading up on fashion trends, taking courses in sewing and design, etc. I also enjoy working with the public, and unlike many sales personnel one meets these days, I consider each customer important and take an interest in her or him.

I hope you find my qualifications suitable for the position I am seeking. I will call you to arrange an interview in the next week or so if I do not hear from you before then.

Sincerely yours,

Jeannetta Quigly

(See accompanying resume page 144.)

PLUME

WORKING WISDOM

(0452)

☐ **THE 100 BEST COMPANIES TO WORK FOR IN AMERICA, by Robert Levering, Milton Moskowitz, and Michael Katz.** This unique guide to excellence rates America's top companies from the employee's point of view, and candid corporate profiles offer inside information you won't find in the employee's handbook. "Should be read by all managers, not just people seeking a job or a job shift."—Thomas J. Peters, co-author of *In Search Of Excellence* (256577—$8.95)

☐ **QUALITY WITHOUT TEARS: The Art of Hassle-Free Management, by Philip B. Crosby.** Pinpoints the "secret enemies" of quality within a company, and shows how quality can be produced without twisting arms and with the full enthusiastic support of fellow executives and the workforce alike. A must for managers, and for every business enterprise. (256585—$8.95)

☐ **RESUMES THAT WORK, by Tom Cowan.** Whether you're a first-job hunter or a career changer, this guide will help you inventory your skills, talents, and past jobs, describe them clearly, and arrange them in the best way suited to your objectives. Like a professional personnel counselor, this comprehensive guide gives you a step-by-step plan—plus numerous sample resumes and cover letters—for formulating the unique job-query approach that will work for you.
(254558—$9.95)

☐ **THE ENTRPRENEURIAL WORKBOOK, by Charlotte Taylor.** Here is a step-by-step guide to starting and operating your own small business that will tell you how to develop a long-range business plan, how to make key start-up decisions, how to find the right personnel, where to go for financing, and more. Plus a model for planning your marketing strategy, and other solutions to typical business problems.
(256607—$9.95)

Prices slightly higher in Canada.

Buy them at your local bookstore or use this convenient
coupon for ordering.

NEW AMERICAN LIBRARY
P.O. Box 999, Bergenfield, New Jersey 07621

Please send me the PLUME BOOKS I have checked above. I am enclosing $_____(please add $1.50 to this order to cover postage and handling). Send check or money order—no cash or C.O.D.'s. Prices and numbers are subject to change without notice.

Name_____

Address_____

City_____State_____Zip Code_____

Allow 4-6 weeks for delivery.
This offer subject to withdrawal without notice.

Plume

EXPERT ADVICE

(0452)

☐ **THE ZURICH AXIOMS Investment Secrets of the Swiss Bankers by Max Gunther.** If conventional investment wisdom is really wise, why isn't everyone rich? A well-known group of Swiss bankers have put together their findings on what really pays off—big—in investing. At last there is nothing secret about how to succeed—Swiss style. (256593—$6.95)

☐ **SURE-THING OPTIONS TRADING A Money-Making Guide to the New Listed Stock and Commodity Options Market by George Angell.** This breakthrough investor's guide makes it easy to understand stock and commodity options and index futures trading. "A good buy for investors who want a solid groundwork to a sophisticated trading tool".—*Futures Magazine* (256143—$7.95)

☐ **THE ENTREPRENEURIAL WORKBOOK by Charlotte Taylor.** Here is a step-by-step guide to starting and operating your own small business that will tell you how to develop a long-range business plan, how to make key start-up decisions, where to go for financing, and more. Plus a model for planning your marketing strategy, and other solutions to typical business problems. (256607—$9.95)

All prices higher in Canada.

Buy them at your local bookstore or use this convenient
coupon for ordering.

NEW AMERICAN LIBRARY
P.O. BOx 999, Bergenfield, New Jersey 07621

Please send me the PLUME BOOKS I have checked above. I am enclosing $_____
(please add $1.50 to this order—no cash or C.O.D.'s. Prices and numbers are subject
to change without notice.

Name_____

Address _____

City_____State_____Zip Code_____

Allow 4-6 weeks for delivery.
This offer subject to withdrawal without notice.

Plume

BUSINESS SAVVY

(0452)

☐ **HOW TO PROMOTE YOUR OWN BUSINESS by Gary Blake and Robert W. Bly.** A practical primer to the ins and outs of advertising and publicity, complete with actual case histories, illustrations, charts, ads and commercials, samples of flyers, brochures, letters and press releases. This is the only promotional guide you'll ever need to make your business a solid success. (254566—$10.95)

☐ **QUALITY WITHOUT TEARS: The Art of Hassle-Free Management by Philip B. Crosby.** Now, from the author of *Quality is Free* comes another must for managers. Crosby pinpoints "the secret enemies" of quality and shows how quality can be produced without twisting arms. "Outstanding . . . brings home the point that no one can afford to blunder along anymore."—*Productivity* (256585—$8.95)

☐ **RESUMES THAT WORK by Tom Cowan.** The complete guide to selling yourself successfully—whether you're seeking your first job, changing jobs, returning to work or changing careers. Includes 126 sample resumes, plus special hints on cover letters and interviews and up-to-date information on the entire spectrum of today's job market. (254558—$9.95)

☐ **WRITING ON THE JOB: A Handbook for Business & Government by John Schell and John Stratton.** The clear, practical reference for today's professional, this authoritative guide will show you how to write clearly, concisely, and coherently. Includes tips on memos, manuals, press releases, proposals, reports, editing and proofreading and much more. (255317—$9.95)

☐ **YOUR GUIDE TO A FINANCIALLY SECURE RETIREMENT by C. Colburn Hardy.** Revised and Updated. Make sure your retirement years are golden. Learn how to set up the best IRA's, how to buy (and avoid) various types of insurance, how to plan your estate, how to invest savings and other ways to make you richer tomorrow—if you start planning today. (256216—$8.95)

All prices higher in Canada.

Buy them at your local bookstore or use this convenient coupon for ordering.

NEW AMERICAN LIBRARY
P.O. Box 999, Bergenfield, New Jersey 07621

Please send me the PLUME BOOKS I have checked above. I am enclosing $_____ (please add $1.50 to this order to cover postage and handling). Send check or money order—no cash or C.O.D.'s. Prices and numbers are subject to change without notice.

Name_____

Address_____

City_____State_____Zip Code_____

Allow 4-6 weeks for delivery.
This offer subject to withdrawal without notice.

Ⓟ Plume

WRITE TO THE TOP

(0452)

☐ **MAGIC WRITING: A Writer's Guide to Word Processing by John Stratton with Dorothy Stratton.** If you are a writer thinking about switching to a word processor, this complete guide will tell you in words you will understand how to choose, master, and benefit from a word proccessor. Plus a computerese-English dictionary and glossary.
(255635—$12.95)

☐ **WRITING ON THE JOB: A Handbook for Business & Government by John Schell and John Stratton.** The clear, practical reference for today's professional, this authoritative guide will show you how to write clearly, concisely, and coherently. Includes tips on memos, mannuals, press releases, proposals, reports, editing and proofreading and much more.
(255317—$9.95)

☐ **THE WRITER'S GUIDE TO MAGAZINE MARKETS: NONFICTION by Helen Rosengren Freedman and Karen Krieger.** 125 top magazines describe the kinds of non-fiction articles they look for—and publish. Included are tips on the best way to prepare and submit your manuscript; the uses of an agent; guidance from writers who've successfully sold pieces; how to negotiate financial terms and rights; awards; grants and contests; plus a glossary of publishing terms and much, much more.
(257956—$9.95)

☐ **THE WRITER'S GUIDE TO MAGAZINE MARKETS: FICTION by Karen Krieger and Helen Rosengren Freedman.** Complete in-depth information on the kinds of short stories 125 top magazines seek—and publish. If you are a short story writer and want to be published, this is the book you owe it to yourself and your work to read.
(257964—$9.95)

Prices slightly higher in Canada.